Italian Nationalism

Enrico Corradini

Translated By Richard Robinson

Sunny Lou Publishing Company
Portland, Oregon, USA
http://www.sunnyloupublishing.com

3rd Edition: July 19, 2025

Original Publication Date: October 19, 2023

ISBN: 978-1-955392-78-5

# # #

This translation from Italian is based on
the Fratelli Treves, Editori, edition of
Il nazionalismo italiano, Milan, 1914.

Contents

Preface..5

Part I...9

I. Principles of Nationalism............................11

II. Proletarian Nations and Nationalism........29

III. The First Nationalist Congress.................51

Part II...69

IV. Democratic Aristocracy and Oligarchic
Democracy 71

V. Liberals and Nationalists............................89

VI. Liberal State and National State............109

VII. Nationalism and Socialism....................131

VIII. Tripolitania, the Balkans, the Turco-
European Plutocracy......................................153

IX. Plutocracy's Satellites.............................159

X. How Democracy Might Depopulate France
....165

XI. On the Eastern Frontier...........................173

XII. The Morality of Productive Possession
....181

XIII. New National Doctrines and Spiritual Renewal...191

XIV. Commemoration of the Battle of Adwa 207

Preface

A portion of this volume includes some pages already published elsewhere, and I have collected them in part through the instinct that compels one to look back over the path just traveled, after having arrived at a certain point along the way.

There are things that preceded the Congress of Florence in December 1910, from which the Nationalist Association emerged. They are connected to the work of individual propaganda that I had begun with several friends of mine, primarily Pier Ludovico Occhini, as far back as 1903, with the founding of *Il Regno*.[1]

The rest of the volume consists, for the most part, of discourses given this year in various cities. And it is a new contribution to the work of review of an entire past and the formation of a entire future that nationalism is assiduously making in Italian politics.

With a humble attitude I offer it primarily to those who persist in saying that they still do not understand, and do not see, what nationalism is made of, or what precisely it is. There is a large number of Italians who conceive of nationalism as *something that stands apart*. One need only make an effort to look for it, and it would be found, but they do not make the effort and for that reason they do not find it, and therefore they continue to say that they do not know

---

[1] *Il Regno*: Italian for *The Kingdom*, a review founded by the Corradini together with the Count Pier Ludovico Occhini (AD 1874-1941), a journalist, writer, and Italian politician.

what it is.

To tell the truth, nothing concerns me more than this *incapacity to pay attention*, which is found in so many parts of the Italian people. Ready to speak, and above all to judge, but unwilling to understand. Readers are familiar with the Italian phrase, spoken with a certain attitude, of "I don't understand this thing!" What they really mean, those who say it, is that the "thing" actually does not exist. And so, for years now, I hear it repeated: "I don't understand nationalism!" And it occurs to me that very few people really believe that they do not understand it because they cannot or because they do not make the effort. It is a common rule that men never doubt their own intelligence, but always the thing that should be understood; but when this rule is applied to nationalism, it is done in a way that exceeds all measure now.

For us, such an incapacity for serious attention and serious reflection in our greater social classes is a holdover of that ethnic debilitation that we suffered after many centuries of bondage and inertia. The fact of the matter is that nationalism is obligated not only to elaborate and expose its own doctrine, but also to create the *public means* of accepting it. For that reason it proceeds initially rather slowly and somewhat cautiously. We have an especial need for this: that the *average liberal public opinion* might become particularly aware that there is a certain difference between liberalism and us, not only in bellicose electoral attitudes, but even more so in the written word, and still even more so in unwritten feelings. We would never want to be *the music of the future* for them, which they sometimes suppose; we would want only to be a somewhat different music, which they are almost never prone to suppose.

However, we are encouraged by younger generations of Italians who are entirely with us and for us, who understand us instinctively, which is much better than just intellectually.

It is for them that the proponents of Italian nationalism carry on their work. One day its importance will seem evident to them. It will ultimately seem clear to them what nationalism is all about. It has to do with expelling from Italy what remains of two foreign revolutions, the Gallic bourgeois revolution and the German socialist revolution; and it has to do with paving the way for an Italian political, moral, and spiritual formation. In other words, sowing in our own soil the seeds of a future civilization of ours that the world might one day nourish itself on.

– March 1914, Florence.

ENRICO CORRADINI

Part I
Before Action

I. Principles of Nationalism[2]

The concept of nationalism is first and foremost founded on the recognition that life is inherently collective in nature. Antisocialists are, in general, considered individualists, but there is a need to clarify in what sense a nationalist or, by natural consequence, an imperialist is an individualist, and in what sense he is exactly the opposite.

A nationalist is an individualist because of the momentary polemic against momentary socialism. He is an individualist in economic matters; but as soon as we leave that behind us and our doctrine becomes clear within, we immediately realize that nationalism is far and away the greatest possible incarnation of anti-individualism that exists in practical reality.

It is not difficult to make it understood that nationalism is a form of collective life. It is, I repeat, the greatest possible form of collective life in practical reality, recognizing that internationalism and humanitarianism are merely two sentimental abstractions, except when they are used as weapons by those who do their utmost to fight in favor of other forms of collective life inferior to that of the nation.

Instead, let us suppose for a moment that the other form of collective life, the so-called socialist

---

[2]Original footnote: from *L'Ombra della vita* [by Enrico Corradini], Ricciardi, Napoli, 1908.

collectivism, was not by now an old fable, and let us see how this collectivism stands in relation to our mode of considering life collectively.

First of all, if socialist collectivism still held any credit, we could demonstrate that it is impossible, simply because human life is collective by nature, and the individual himself is none other than the product of a momentary arrangement of collective acts and deeds, from nutrition to culture. This collective state of humanity needs to be looked at closely. I, an individual, at this moment in time, as much to say a momentary particle, in all that I am, and how I dress, and how I eat and speak and what I know and feel and think, I am the product of a collective life that from the present moment extends into the past, just as from the present it will extend into the future. There is the atmosphere in which everything breathes, the earth from which everything obtains its nutrition, the chain of generative acts through generations, whereby everything comes into being; and these are the actual conditions under one aspect that is real and under another that is figurative (symbolic, as is commonly said) of the collective life that each of us partakes in. When the wind blows on the surface of the sea, all the waves that succeed one another, from the horizon to the beach, are free and finite in themselves, but they are all born of the sea and all die in the sea. Individuals are the same with respect to the collective life: free and finite in themselves, but they are all are born of the collective life and all die in it. The sea of collective life is an entity with respect to individuals just as the sea itself is an entity with respect to the waves. And if we needed another proof, we should consider that there are functions that are *ad libitum*[3] for the individual and not of primary necessity except for the collective life: procreation, for example.

All this is easy to understand. But, precisely for this reason, it is not given to men to put hope in socialist collectivism. And why not? Simply because such collectivism, if it had the possibility of existing, would strive to collectivize life at the scale of the individual, while life collectivizes by transcending the individual, that is, by producing greater organisms, greater forms of essential being. Socialist collectivism starts with the concept of equality: equal men, equal harnesses of work, equal work, equal pay; the men of one generation equal to the men of another, in conditions that are always equal; as much to say, in the ideal collectivist regime, we will have quantities of men succeeding one another, generation after generation, and always incapable of amounting to anything more than the possibility of a man. Life, on the contrary, starts with the fact of diversity, and with an always greater diversity it tends to compose, throughout generations, always greater unities. The works of collective life are the city, the nation, empire, arts, civilization. The Roman Empire was, in the Occident, the greatest unity of collective life, and as such it is sacred in men's memory. When Napoleon I is crowned emperor, the crown stands above the apogee of the collective life of Gallic, Roman, Germanic, Monarchic, Revolutionary France, formed for one moment in perfect unity. The *Divine Comedy* is a true and proper work of collective life, the greatest unity of ideal collective life that has appeared in the Occident.

---

[3] *Ad libitum*: Latin for "optional."

Masterpieces of art are, throughout the centuries, true and proper collective formations. Centuries prepare the way for them before the artists, other centuries develop them afterwards, and those who think that the *Divine Comedy* was born as such entirely from Dante's head understand very little. He created something that all generations add to. So-called progress is a collective work. And we become more aware of it when the idea that followers of public opinion have of it today is abandoned; the idea, that is, of an indefinite path that humanity takes toward its perfection. This idea is arbitrary, sentimental, and gross, and is actually an error; because that indefinite path does not exist, and the only thing that exists are some fields in which humanity progresses, and others in which it turns back. Thus the Greeks were in advance of us in the moral sciences and in the arts, and we are in advance of the Greeks in the physical sciences and in their application to the needs of material life. What is needed, instead of the idea of progress, is to put forward the idea of integration. Every age, every civilization, every people, every family of working-class people add their contribution to this integration of living humanity throughout the centuries. From one epoch to the next a new aspect of humanity is revealed or, better, is created. It is one province added to another province in order to create the territory of an empire that always extends itself. Thus the Greeks added the province of the moral sciences and the arts, as I have said; the Romans, law and war; the moderns, sciences and their inventions. And all these aspects that the living history of humanity integrates with, all these provinces of interminable empire, have equal value. And to believe differently is an error, or a delusion.

We delude ourselves because, immersed in our time, we think with the brain of our time. Thus, today the idea of progress is identified with the idea of the progress of the feeling of human solidarity, or piety, and the like. This solidarity is even confused with civilization, which is something so much vaster and more complex. It is a delusion that comes from our being immersed in our time. There is in our time this verbal optimism of human solidarity, and because of it we are drawn to reason in the following way: we have a feeling of human solidarity that is greater than the ancients; in this feeling consists civilization; ergo, we are more civilized than the ancients. One reasons poorly. We are more and less civilized than the ancients. Or rather, we are neither more nor less. We are we, and the ancients are the ancients, and between the two we make up humanity.

Now, turning to the collective nature of life, we see that this appears more clearly in its political forms.

That said, one understands perfectly well what ought to be understood by nationalism. Nationalism is the doctrine of those who consider the nation as the greatest unity of collective life, like a true and proper greater individual. Nationalism rests on two principles: 1st, life is constructed in time and space beyond individual limits; 2nd, the constructive virtue of great collectivities that is placed in the species cannot go beyond a certain limit, and this limit is indicated by the borders of nations and their empires. As much to say, nations and their empires are greater constructions that can subsist in the reality of events; and that would be evident in and of itself if a certain mode of believing in internationalism and in the future union of all humanity did not perdure. It is said: as from the city we arrived at the nation, so from the nation we will arrive at the union of nations. It is a logical analogy that hides some factual errors. First of all, nations are historical facts that occurred and occur; a nation is a geographical fact, it is a climatic fact, it is an ethnic fact: the value of race is disputed in the composition of a people, but there is no disputing the mixture of blood, the diverse composition of diverse blood that makes up the Italians, the French, the Spanish, the Germans, the English, and so on, each different from the other. Moreover the nation is, strictly speaking, a historical fact, a fact of language, a fact of culture, a fact of politics. France's having had a monarchy that centralized everything makes it different from Italy, which until recently was divided into regions. Now, in the face of this combination of facts, internationalism remains a purely logical deduction made by mistaken analogy.

But then the same causes that created the nation from the city prevent us from believing in the union of all nations. For they emerged not because of one force only, but two; that is, a force of development from the interior toward the exterior, of always greater association and cohesion, and also a force of struggle against [pressure from] the exterior. More than the will of the men of a country, the will of foreigners have created the nation through war, invasions, expulsions; and it is probable that no nation would have arisen on earth without struggles from the exterior, because without this there would have been no need to unify, there would have been no need for an energetic like-minded will, and revolutions would have resulted in always greater disunion, or inertia in always greater corruption and debilitation. Nations have emerged because they had an antagonist, and in a certain way they are nothing else than the consolidation of a permanent state of war, of the ones against the others. And behold two forces that contemporaneously act in life: a force of association (an alliance of similar elements for a common defense) and a force of conflict. Suppress the conflict and you suppress life. Man either stands on his own two feet to fight, or he lies down a cadaver and becomes infested with worms. In other words, human life is by its very nature dramatic. Now, the union of all peoples (against whom?), while suppressing the antagonist in the drama, would suppress the drama itself; suppressing the conflict would suppress life; or rather, it would refocus the battle to within each country. Do we want to be in a state of perpetual revolution? Let us cultivate pacifism. One can imagine all the states of the world united, but then suppose every state broken down into so many municipalities, and every one of these a nest of vipers. The nation is far and away the best thing humanity has created, having found itself stuck between the two instincts of association and conflict. The nation is the imperfect realization of the law that nature puts forward: an internal peace for an external war. When an internal war is wanted, people become pacifists.

All that is evident, and it would be superfluous to mention if it weren't, I repeat, the fashion of internationalism. You hear serious people saying

"Humanity marches toward the union of all peoples."
Well, humanity does not march at all, and the truly
modern man, the new man rather, is recognized by his
disregard for similar sentimental idealisms, by similar
real and characteristic maladies of the spirit. They are
the moralities of our time and one must know how to
disregard them. And we must be realistic and have realistic ideals. It seems that these last two words are at
odds, but only when they are united, when they form
a whole that is endowed with a noble intent and worthy of high honor. Only when it is realistic, when, that
is, it is based on fact, is idealism worthy of this holy
name, and we need to stop calling everything that is
no more than a caricature, that is no more than the re-
sounding expressions of the charlatanism of the century, by the same term. If these are ideals, we need to
learn how to live without ideals. But I say that the
greatness of one's nation is the true idealism, while
internationalism is, as with many other similar doctrines, a false idealism. It is a dogma of the new secular, humanitarian religion. One needs to know cor-
dially how to disregard these dogmas and these religions. Nationalism is also, over and above everything
else, the return to a realistic conception of the world.
New, real men are realists.

And what is there, finally, of the realistic in
internationalism? There is the cosmopolitanism of the
educated classes and there are families of people at
the same point of civilization. To be sure, as long as
the necessity of the antagonist consents to it, humanity tends to go outside national borders and to form
larger corporations of nations, like, for example,
Western Europe today. Several nations collaborate to

create a civilization. But it is an illusion to believe that this is a first big step towards internationalism, considered as a certain future arrangement of all human society. And we are victims of this illusion because we find ourselves immersed in our time, and we cannot without difficulty think with a free mind. But civilizations are momentary states of equilibrium among multiple peoples, which fall apart in a way that is extremely easier than those other momentary states of equilibrium among various classes of a single people who call themselves a nation. Is it possible to conceive of a civilization without any more revolutions? No. So, civilizations without any more war are also impossible to conceive of. Wars are revolutions within the confines of a civilization (when they are not among multiple civilizations each armed against the other, or between a civilization and barbarians), just as revolutions are nothing else than wars within the confines of a nation. It is well to remind revolutionary pacifists of this.

Now, is it necessary to add that imperialism is the natural consequence of nationalism? To recognize this is equivalent to recognizing the useful function of war. But one runs up against two other dogmas, or moralities, of contemporary religion: the inviolability of human life and pacifism. Eh, well, one needs to go back to elementary reflection and consider that human life loses its value immediately as it passes from the individual state to the collective one; and the morality of the inviolability of human life is a true and proper immorality because it aims to put a price on what does not have any: it is individual egoism that defrauds collective altruism. But from a national point of view the individual has no more importance than a drop of water compared to the sea, than a leaf that falls from the tree with respect to a forest that were as large as the earth. On this truth, or morality actually, war is based, which in an individual state of mind cannot really be understood; soldiers from the collective state (an army that fights), when they return to the individual state (panic fear), they no longer understand it and flee, and all other people who are incapable of passing from the individual state to the collective state condemn it. And war is truly an evil, but a necessary evil, as it is also an evil necessity, and all of life is nothing more than a back and forth between these two producers of events commonly called good and evil. And one should know that he who does evil, great evil, like war, for the terrible need of men, represents what is most tragically sacred in the world. The Roman reapers of lives are sacred. Napoleon is sacred. Conquerors are under the sanctity of fate. In reality, war is nothing but a necessity for nations that are or tend to be imperialistic, when they don't tend to perish, according to the eternal verse by Dante which everyone knew: *Perchè una gente impera e l'altra langue*.[4] Wars are necessary like revolutions, the external and internal imperialism of nations, two imperialisms that make up the entire history of humanity, since the world is what it is. The entire world is imperialistic either externally or internally, and today there is an imperialism of proletarians that calls itself socialism. The entire world is imperialistic, and the state of the globe is nothing but an imperialism of men over other living beings and things. Do

---

[4]*Perchè una gente impera e l'altra langue*. Italian for "Because one people rules and another languishes." Dante, *Inferno*, 7.82.

we not believe ourselves to be first among the animals? Anthropomorphism is an aspect of this imperialism, which extends as far as heaven and creates Olympus. Morality is nothing else than another aspect of the same imperialism. The entire world is imperialistic because the entire world, as we have mentioned, is constructed in time and space, beyond individual limits, and you knock down these limits in order to create classes, nations, empires; and the inviolability of human life, and pacifism, are consequently to be relegated to old fables, in the patrimony of the sentimental idealism of men of the past. It is important to remember that contempt for death is the greatest factor of life. And amidst these herds of sheep and clever good-for-nothings that make up the so-called ruling classes in Italy today, give me a hundred men who are ready to die, and Italy is renewed.

But if it is important always to be imperialistic in doctrine, one cannot always be, and must never be, like that in practice, in a certain period of the nation to which one belongs; otherwise, one becomes, contrariwise, abstract windbags, like those we mentioned earlier. Imperialism is an actual state of the nation and cannot be forced by theory. It is a state of exuberance, vitality, force, work and production, industry, commerce, money. And it is more difficult, for example, to make a nation imperialistic externally when it is afflicted internally by a class imperialism; and only when the latter is victorious and full of energy, or conquered, only then does the natural period of the other begin, i.e., true and proper external imperialism. Also, history teaches us that the two imperialisms can be contemporaneous, and in fact the one seems to foster the other. However, wars are necessary for the one, just as revolutions are for the other. And in Italy today, there are some who think that a revolution would be more useful, which would sweep away these ruling classes, these avid and inept clientelists that we have hanging about our necks. In twenty years from now, if not sooner, Italy will be entirely imperialistic. Of course, Italy aside, the world was never prepared to be imperialistic like it is today. Nationalism and imperialism are two true forms of life suited for this gigantic modern world, vast, powerful, and fast-moving beyond words. This greater instrument of human history, the nation, seems to be ideally suited for creating the greatest history in the vastness of the modern world. There is nothing seemingly better able to give a proper idea of what human actions are capable of today than the great empires of contemporary nations. The earth will see empires as it has never seen them before. New artists already perceive them and base their style on them.

What will the new style be? Does nationalism and imperialism have their own style, their own esthetic? To be honest, I do not have a ready-made theory on this topic, and I have no idea what might happen in China, or in Spain, but it appears to me that if Italy one day succeeds in becoming a real and proper nation with its colonies, with a valorous and victorious political life amidst the peace and war of other nations, on that day, it appears to me, the flower of its art must be classical in style. I have sustained on other occasions that classicism is not specific to some people alone, as if it were a privilege of race or blood, but can belong to all peoples who are capable of arriving at a special spiritual state of mind. Classicism is a state of mind of humanity in general, and not an ethnic characteristic. But now I want to forget what I have written on other occasions, and I want to focus on asserting only this: that classicism is inborn with us Italians, who were profoundly Hellenized at first, and Romanized later.

But it is necessary to understand immediately what we mean by this. It is necessary to understand what classicism in ancient art consists in, and to see that it consists in a particular feeling about life whereby, among all things, it assumes an importance beyond comparison to those things that can be raised to their greatest level of energy as forces, and to their greatest level of harmony as forms. Classicism is all right there. It is a form of imperialism. It is the vigor of forces up to and including victory, and the harmony of forms whose harmony is also a victory and is called beauty. When a Greek artist takes an athlete from reality and makes of him the model of agonistic beauty in sculpture; when he takes the warrior and makes a hero out of him; when he takes a man and makes an Olympic god, what in the world is he doing? He is making something that is a true and proper act of faith according to the greatest of religions inscribed in the heart of man; this faith: that humanity and nature can, in an admirably beautiful form, become God. This is the real and proper classicism that is the art of triumph, of celebration, the art of aristocracy, and I do not mean here only the aristocracy of birth, but also those better aristocracies that emerge from time to time from the deep tumultuous bosom of a democracy worthy of the name. To such classicism

which is the harmony of wisdom and beauty in
Greece, worldly Rome added two other spirits: the
spirit of power and the spirit of vastness. Rome was
the first in the West to open up all the vastness with
its power. And such a harmonious, beautiful, powerful classicism on a grand scale was transfused into
our blood after eighteen centuries of atavism and culture.

On the other hand, non-classical art, the art
that we can call Romantic, is born by denying to life
the virtue of winning. Romantic is that which is afflicted in its baseness and in its misery and that which
imprecates unbeautifully. The Greek statue has before
it the path that leads from this earth to Olympus; today's statue has no path before it and, forgive me for
saying so, it remains where it fell in the tears of that
nonentity who gave it its image.

That said, one understands better why, hoping
for a victorious Italy, I hope for a return to real classical art. But let us be clear: it must be an art not by imitation, but by creation; that is, an art that is born of a
feeling about life as classical artists had, but with a
modern spirit. For example, the Belgian sculptor Con-
stantin Meunier is a classical artist by creation,
whereas the monument that is erected to Victor Em-
manuel II in Rome is classical only by imitation. Con-
stantin Meunier in a classical state of mind, that is,
with the religious faith that a man's virtue together
with his strength can attain victory, has created the
standard of modern artwork; while the architect of the
Roman monument through study and reminiscences
simply re-builds what has already been built. His

monument is classical and Roman in its vastness, but it is derivative and does not bear the sign of its times. He is a scholar in whose mind an act of memory has been attained, while Meunier is a religious in whose spirit the rite of transfiguration of modern life and the worker has been attained through great love. And into Meunier's work has passed the deafening torrent of modern life, while it does not pass into the Roman monument; that torrent whose voice can and must pass as much into a poem as into a monument that is as high as a hill, as into a statue. The important thing is that the torrent's voice pass into that new classical art of ours.

Of this torrent of modern life, from the swollen river and impetuous course, as never before seen – today man cannot do without the religion and faith of its victorious forces. Rome was the first empire on earth to mention the word vastness. Something today reconnects us to Rome, ourselves made even vaster thereby. Our great modern roadways gain strength alongside the great Roman roads. The modern world appears to be a development of the ancient Roman one that made the Mediterranean sea its lake. There is in the Roman proconsuls and legionnaires who cross all mountains and seas the true direct ancestor of the modern man, an ancestor with an equal spirit but only slower vehicles. Our history starts with Rome; all great roads lead from Rome, and from Rome all great nations have their origin. And Roman history is but the first chapter of our European history. In the name of our Rome, if we Italians return to feel the virtue of this city, our classical art will rise again, in a victorious Italy, in the modern world. And it will be a simple and ingenuous art like today's rude force; it will have the gift of sobriety and brevity according to the necessity that we have today to get straight to the point; it will be grandiose and powerful, just as the world around us is grandiose and powerful.

And our religion? Magnificent is the religion of heroes and nature.

Do readers remember the salutation of the God Mithras celebrated in ancient Persia? The celebration went like this. The procession to go and greet the God gathered well before dawn. The High Priests came first, followed by a long line of magi, in immaculate white robes, who sang hymns and carried the sacred fire in silver thuribles. They were followed by three hundred sixty-five youths dressed in scarlet who represented the days of the year and the color of fire. Next came the chariot of the Sun, empty, decorated with garlands, pulled by white horses barded in pure gold. Then came a white horse of majestic stature whose face scintillated in gems, in honor of Mithras. Immediately after came the king in a chariot of ivory inlaid with gold, followed by personages of the royal family, all in embroidered costumes, and by a long procession of nobles, riding on richly-embroidered camels. This magnificent cortege, moving toward the East, ascended Mount Oronte by slow steps, and, arrived at the summit, the High Priest put on the tiara garlanded with myrtle. And he saluted the first rays of the nascent sun with incense and prayer. The other magi gradually joined in with him, singing hymns to Ormuzd, the fountain of all blessings, from whom

Mithras, the radiant, was sent to bring joy on earth and to conserve the principle of life. Finally everyone united in a universal chorus of praise, while the king, princes, and nobles prostrated themselves before the day star.

In our consciousness there is an aspiration, which one cannot fail to acknowledge, an aspiration for a religion that instills in us the feeling of nature such as the salutation of Mithras did, combined with the cult of heroes, in other words with that part of humanity that has lived on this earth in order to create on high the kingdom of the eternal human ideal.

II. Proletarian Nations and Nationalism[5]

There is a need to explain again, o ladies and gentlemen, there is a need to explain again the word "nationalism."

Many persist in retaining that nationalism is the same as patriotism, and that a nationalist is the same as a good Italian.

If this were so, we would still need to explain what patriotism means, and what it means to be a good Italian.

Now, we do not believe that we are far from the truth by asserting that what follows is the *commonly held* meaning of the two words. A good Italian, or patriot, is a good citizen who practices his profession honestly and profitably, lives with a legitimate wife and healthy children in a comfortable house, pays his taxes dutifully, and every time he is reminded of the fatherland, of Italy, he exclaims: "O, dear Italy, dear fatherland!" And during national solemnities he is moved, above all if he has obtained recently, or soon plans to obtain, the Knight's Cross. The good Italian, in a word, is the blood brother of the perfect bourgeois who says: "Give me comfort, and I will allow myself some luxury as well; a luxury of feeling: patriotism."

---

[5]Original footnote: A discourse given in January 1911, in Naples, Florence, Venice, Padua, Verona, and Arezzo.

Eh, well, nationalism is something different.

Of course, we too want to be good Italians, and if patriotism means love of the fatherland, we too are patriots. We have a devouring love of the fatherland. We want to reawaken the love of the fatherland like a spark that starts a fire. We have, in fact, made our love of the fatherland our religion. Of this dear mother, Italy, we love what is, what was, and what will be. We have gone out to find our Italian brothers beyond the Ocean, and when they were sleeping, tired from the fatigues of the day, we, in the dead of the night, in the endless solitudes of the *haciendas*, we stayed awake to examine the books, and, their wages seeming to us to be scarce, we felt grief, as if it were a disappointment that had touched us personally. We have gone out to find our Italian brothers on the other side of the brief sea, and we have spoken together of a common hope, and as soon as one of them wept, we made a vow for those tears.

But for all that, nationalism is something different from patriotism. It is, rather, in a certain way, just the opposite. Nationalism is the opposite of patriotism.

I will explain.

Patriotism is altruistic, nationalism is egoistic. The perfect bourgeois does not enjoy hearing us acknowledge our egoism, because everything we have is different from them, and above all the egoism. But nationalism is certainly egoistic. It is the egoism of citizens with respect to the nation. And, moreover, what need is there for many explanations? Do you not, ladies and gentlemen, hear the difference in the two words themselves, "fatherland"[6] and "nation"? When we wish to express our love of Italy, we say "fatherland"; when we wish to assert the power of Italy, we say "nation." Well, nationalism is the plant growing from this root; it is, in other words, the development of the initial sense of power contained in the word "nation." And by power is meant the power to benefit the nation itself, the entire people, the entire citizenry. And this is why I said that nationalism is egoistic and is, therefore, in that light, the opposite of patriotism, which is always altruistic. Because nationalism considers the nation as a power to benefit the citizenry. The patriot, on the other hand, if he is a true patriot, like our liberating fathers, not like those mentioned above, the patriot renders a service to the fatherland, and until his dying day, if it should come to that, until his dying day!

Do we want to know more?

Let's think about class.

What is class for the proletariat that works?

It is certainly also an object of love. The worker loves his class. There is a class spirit, a real and proper spirit of belonging. But above all, the worker is stimulated, in his relations with class, by an egotistical calculation: by means of class he wants to obtain his economic betterment. Class is a means, a weapon, a combatant army for the economic betterment of the proletariat. Class is, finally, the power of

---

[6]Fatherland: the word in Italian for fatherland is "*patria*," from which comes the word patriotism.

the proletariat to wage class warfare.

Well, according to nationalism, the Italian nation must be the power, the army, the weapon, the means; it must, finally, be the great unity of all the forces that must fight for the economic betterment of all Italians.

But someone might object that class is a much simpler concept, that it is a lesser unity of homogenous forces. I reply that class, when one is talking about "the working class," "the working proletariat," is in reality a composite of classes, classes that often have a conflict of interests. Those forces in conflict exist even while there is a State that seeks to moderate and coordinate them; and they would have more conflict still if the State did not exist and the classes were left alone to fight amongst themselves over their interests. Only, among the reasons for conflict, a reason for solidarity between the classes was also discovered to exist. It was discovered that the classes, besides their particular interests in conflict, had also a common interest: they had to obtain a benefit that was common to everyone, their economic betterment, to be precise. And for this reason they came together as one single class. And in the struggle, and through the struggle itself, their solidarity became so cemented that those that were in reality multiple classes always appeared really as one single class anymore, and their conflicting interests, the more they were concealed, the more their common interests stood out. But the class is in reality a composite of classes, and their conflicting interests exist.

One might still object that socialism is easy

and nationalism is difficult. Socialism is easy because it is clear, and it is clear because it is precise. The worker when he participates in the class struggle knows precisely, sees precisely, that he struggles for himself and not for others. There is nothing that stands between him and the adversary that he struggles with. And the adversary is precise. And the goal of the struggle is precise: it is an increase in daily wages. In nationalism, on the other hand, nothing is precise, nothing is clear, and nothing therefore is easy. Is that so? It is so. But I say to you, o gentlemen, that a thing, when it is difficult, is not for this reason any less necessary, nor less useful, nor less important, nor less great, nor less beautiful, and it is actually, on the contrary, true. I say to you that, in our historical period, for transitory reasons, for the same exact class struggle, we have lost sight of the truth that even for all the citizens of a nation, beneath their innumerable conflicts of interest, a common interest exists, a real and proper economic betterment to be held in common, a real and proper increase in daily wages. And I will prove it to you with an example. With an example of French and English citizens who, for the single fact that the one is English and the other French, have one economic condition that the Italian at an equal position in society does not have. And therefore the French and the English, when they feel national solidarity, they feel something that is in line with their interest, precisely like the proletarian worker who feels something that is in line with his interest when he feels class solidarity.

Germany lodged itself with its influence in the heart of the Turkish empire, at Constantinople, and it launched the proposal of the Bagdad railroad, a long bridge from Constantinople through Asia Minor to the Persian Gulf. Having found the Russians hostile to the idea, it succeeded in reconciling itself with Russia, and the two proceeded to move forward together with the grand design. As for England, Germany spilling over into the Persian Gulf with its railroad will wound it in the side, in its Indian empire. So Germany continues its conquering march to the East. The Bagdad railroad will be the path of its new commercial expansion. Its traveling salesmen will pass over it and invade the East; its products will be carried on it, and they will invade the East. And an incalculable wealth will pass in the opposite direction, from the East to Germany; an incalculable wealth that will be enjoyed by individuals, and by all the classes, even the proletariat, of the Germanic empire. Thus a state, an empire, an emperor enact a truly national, doubly national, form of politics: first, because it is done not by individuals, but by the German nation in the unity of its forces; second, because its beneficial effects, its products, will be distributed among all German individuals.

Now, ladies and gentlemen, you no longer need to ask me in what struggle does national solidarity involve itself: in the international class struggle; I have already given you the example of Germany; in the international class struggle which in ordinary times, and mild words, is called international competition, and in extraordinary times, with strong words, is called war.

And this is the central, fundamental thought of

nationalism.

Nationalism is an attempt to shift the problem of national life from internal to external politics.

Nationalism asserts this list of truths:

1. the conditions of life of one nation are coordinated with those of other nations;
2. for some nations this coordination is subordination, dependency, economic and moral dependency, even if no political dependency exists;
3. Italy is precisely one of those nations that depend economically and morally on others, although for fifty years now it has ceased its political dependency;
4. this dependency of Italy is extremely serious; and lastly;
5. Italy must free itself from this economic and moral dependency, as it has already freed itself from that political one, because it can and it should.

By just analogy, for the love of verbal efficiency and clarity, and in order to show how much nationalism responds to the spirit of our time, I call those nations proletarian that, like Italy, are in a state of dependency. So the proletariat, according to socialism, was and still is in a state of dependency on the bourgeois class.

And continuing by analogy, I add that nationalism wants to be for the entire nation what socialism was for the single proletariat. What was socialism for the proletariat? An attempt at redemption in part, and within the limits of the possible it succeeded. And what does nationalism want to be for the nation? An attempt at redemption, and, God willing, may it succeed to the fullest.

Days ago, dear gentlemen, I found myself in Rome; and in journalistic and political circles I was speaking with friends who caught me up on Italy's external policies of the moment. Friends told me that Italy would have taken steps in Vienna to know Austria's intention with respect to the renewal of the alliance, and Vienna this time would have shown a closed reserve; and then Italy would have turned to Paris to assay the terrain around the possibility of a future alliance with France; but even Paris would have shown reserve and ill will. So Italy could have only one perspective before its eyes: that of standing alone. The news arrived that Turkey, to Italy's harm, had begun to favor an Austro-German penetration, backed by American capital, in Tripolitania. And a friend, with respect to Tripolitania, added something that I cannot repeat because I gave him my word that I would keep it a secret. But it is something that if it were true, as it seems certain to be, if in Tripolitania it were confirmed to be true, a fact that is almost certified – if this should be the case, o ladies and gentlemen, the terrible fact of the matter is that all of Sicily would be starved because of it.[7]

---

[7]Original footnote: We said this in January, and, on February 11, *il Secolo,* in a correspondence from Tripoli, published this:

> *Cyrenaica is a region rich in sulphur, whose deposits it is said are far and away superior to those of Sicily. Now it is announced that the*

Well, I don't guarantee the exactness of the news; but I do guarantee the profound sense of desolation that it gave me; I guarantee the profound sense of desolation that I discovered, several days ago, as mentioned, in the journalistic and political circles of Rome, similar to what I felt two years earlier when Austria threatened us with war and annexed Bosnia

---

Americans, who are presently doing those archaeological digs in Cyrenaica which were denied to Italy (which had to content itself with reconstructing the network of ancient Roman roads), had obtained the concession of exploitation of the sulphur mines. Given the abundance of this material in Cyrenaica and its existence in vast outcrops that make the work of excavating it proceed more quickly, it is anticipated that the quantity of mineral soon to be dumped on the market will diminish in no small measure the Sicilian exportation and greatly affect the economic conditions of the island where so many thousands of people have food on the table because of the sulphur industry.

And *Il Secolo* commented:

Let us bring the readers' attention back to this correspondence of ours, or rather to a really important point. That Turkey would have conceded to an American labor syndicate the mining of sulphur in Cyrenaica is a fact that was already something we were aware of, and its seriousness cannot escape anyone: nor can the deductions that our correspondent draws from it be said to be illogical or exaggerated. Readers will ask in what does our so-called economic penetration of Tripolitania consist, if we let the major economic advantages of the country be exploited by others. The blame is given perhaps in part to our financiers' diffidence, hesitation, lack of initiative: but

and Herzegovina. I guarantee the profound sense of desolation that those news items awakened in me.

It is with such great desolation that we think of the current state of our fatherland in its relations with other nations. The news can be false, but we are always with tightened heart prepared to receive such news and, if that were possible, worse news; so bad is the state in which, we know, our fatherland finds itself. We feel threatened, and we do not feel in any way protected by those who ought to be protecting us. I mean that each one of us knows, each one of us feels in his heart, each one of us sees with his eyes and touches with his hand, in what an extreme state of destitution it has been reduced, after so many years of continual and progressive degeneration, the entire body of political personnel responsible for handling our foreign affairs.

In parliament recently, while our current min-

_____

above all to the inability of our government, which would have, in certain cases, the duty of overseeing, knowing, anticipating, and also soliciting private competition when it comes to business, which the general interests of the country can feel the accomplishment of or not. In the present case, the American economic penetration... in Tripoli constitutes a very grave setback for us...

Precisely. But these sorts of setback, we will always have them as long as the sole norm of external and colonial policy will be that of peaceful penetration and nothing more. And of a peaceful penetration that does not happen. The fact is, then, a confirmation of the nationalist law -- that many internal questions are resolved by questions of external policy: the situation in Sicily can be made worse than it now is, internally, by a matter of external politics.

ster of foreign affairs was exposing his budget, a deaf
murmur ran several times through the banks of the
deputies, the same deputies who have so little national feeling. It was a murmur of rebellion against the
minister's words, of such rebellion that the more his
report shocked his listeners, the more they broke out
in open disapproval. The instinct of national preservation, like the instinct of personal preservation felt in
an individual before the threat of some misfortune;
the instinct of national preservation, in the same parliament, manifested itself in that way. "At a certain
point," a deputy with a generous heart, a friend of
mine, said to me, "at a certain point, hearing that minister, and knowing so much misery of the soul, so
much abandonment, I felt a shudder run through my
body! I thought that it was Italy I was listening to, our
fatherland, given its many interests and its dignity en-
trusted to that man!"

Well, gentlemen, how many Italians today,
reawakened, feel the same tragic shudder!

For historical reasons, and this is not the place
to go it into now, this admirable Italian people, which
has barely half a century of national existence, has
fallen into the hands of a political personnel that is "at
the end the line," already in decomposition.

Think now; unfold a map of Europe before
your eyes, and look at it from the perspective of our
Latin sister.

What is France to us? It is our metropolis. It
has the monopoly of Latin civilization, and everything that is Italian, in Italy and abroad, from Rome to

Buenos Aires, passes under its yoke. In the kingdom of civilization, we are a tributary province of the neighboring republic.

What is more, this country, which had already occupied Algeria, extended its reach closer to us and below us and took Tunisia away as well, closed us off from that side. Look in the other direction, towards Austria. The Italian lands that it possesses, they are becoming more and more, in its hands, a barrier against us. Those brothers of ours, the last dead sentinels of Italianity, resist as best they can with their language, their culture, the stones of their city, which still carry, but in vain, the signs of the Eagle and the Lion. Austria squeezes them with greater and greater barbarousness in the last defenses; it squeezes them and it squeezes us, especially since it throws on them and on us, almost crushing them and us, the mass of its new conquest, Bosnia and Herzegovina.

This is what happened: whereas we did not want conquest and hated the politics of adventure, others practiced the politics of adventure and made conquests around us, to our harm. We said no to Egypt, and we have said no multiple times to Tripoli. And Egypt is now England's, and France conquered Tunisia. Austria conquered Bosnia and Herzegovina. England and France have gobbled up the best of Tripoli, which should have been ours. In Tripoli, as I mentioned, the Austro-Germans penetrate. Germany dominates in the Balkan East, it dominates in Constantinople. Austria takes the upper hand in our sea, and even in the port of Venice; it is even, it is said, waving its flag over the Lago di Garda. The enormous pan-Germanism descends from the septentrion, already instigates the Tyrol against our Trentino, is already at the gates of Austrian Trieste. Austria itself has been made its instrument of conquest. The same poorly restored Turkey turns against us, and it arms Tripoli which, at one time, we did not want to take away from it.

The circle of conquering nations, the economic circle and the moral circle, is tightening its grip around us, and we nourished ourselves on renunciations because of philosophical utopianism, popular blindness, and bourgeois cowardice.

Can we break it, this circle?

For now we pass over it.

And how?

By emigration.

Ladies and gentlemen, whatever you think about emigration, and whatever you were told, think again!

Emigration is a dispersion of our people into all parts of the world, onto a foreign soil, among foreign peoples, under a foreign legislation. Do not judge it only by the enrichment of a few individuals, nor by the millions [of lira] that emigrants send back to the fatherland. Judge it also from a national point of view, and understand that emigration is, if you allow me to say so, an anti-imperialism of servitude.

This condition of emigration, the need that so many millions of Italians have to look for bread and work beyond the ocean; and the other condition, of the circle of other nations closing in on us, have made me, by analogy, call Italy a proletarian nation.

And if we now recall yet another condition, of the political personnel who govern us, we see that Italy can be compared to the proletariat before social-ism came along to redeem it. There exists in national organs, in the organs of thought, will, action, the same extreme debility as the proletariat had before its redemption. The proletariat, in the darkness of its ig-norance, hadn't the least idea even that it could, by means of struggling, organize itself, transform itself, and redeem itself. And Italy, in the ignorance of its political personnel, did not have an equal footing. Na-tionalism came to shed the first light. Nationalism as-serted the necessity of international struggle, so that the nation can take its economical and moral place in the world.

Nationalism first and foremost asserted Italy's necessity to form a national consciousness, which is, it too, a bodily spirit; it is a spirit of solidarity amongst its citizens, just as consciousness of class is the spirit of solidarity amongst the workers that I cel-ebrated earlier.

Must we demonstrate that national conscious-ness is lacking in Italy?

It is superfluous.

We must begin to mutate the colors in the pic-ture and speak more comforting things, because we must have faith in the future of our fatherland.

We must therefore research instead the reasons why Italy does not have a developed national consciousness and begin immediately to recognize that it does not, because it cannot.

And it cannot for the following reasons:

1. Italy, in short, o gentlemen, until yesterday, was never a nation.

2. It did not have, and does not have, even a national language, except in literature.

3. Italy was made by a small war and a small revolution.

4. Italy was made by many different groups, often in antagonism amongst themselves: official, aristocratic, and bourgeois monarchism; popular Garibaldism; cosmopolitan Mazzinianism. And later even they endured, and they still endure, these antagonists.

5. Italy was made by too many diplomatic tricks and turns, and by foreign arms.

6. Italy too quickly descended into class warfare, and the initial formation of its consciousness was arrested. And ultimately,

7. Italy fell and could not help falling, for the small revolution whereby it was made; it fell into the hands of the political personnel that I mentioned earlier, and which was and is the remnant of servile times, the extreme remnant of traditions, methods, a people already in the process of degeneration and decomposition at

that time, at the head of minuscule govern-
ments, both weak and inept.

Having recognized this, nationalism asserts itself as the educator of national consciousness. Or, to
put it another way, it asserts itself (let us say another
comforting thing!), it asserts itself as the mark of
progress, in Italy, of an unhoped-for progress with respect to the formation of a national consciousness.

Nationalism has begun to develop this consciousness as an activity.

The old patriot, the good, perfect, bourgeois
Italian whom we spoke of at the beginning, had a
false patriotism, false because false, but primarily because inactive. It was a dead patriotism. Now, on the
other hand, nationalism is a living patriotism.

National consciousness today is conceived of
as a religious consciousness: fertile in works.

It is conceived of as a product of activity and
at the same time as a productive activity.

It is conceived of as informative of all the life
of the citizen.

The Italian people, o gentlemen, lack discipline. Must we demonstrate it? It is superfluous. Let's
not occupy ourselves so much with the individual.
But the individual as seen in public services, in public
offices. Eh, well, it is superfluous to demonstrate just
how much discipline in public services and offices the
Italian citizen lacks. Just how much of a sense of duty
he lacks.

Now, national consciousness, such as nationalism conceives of it, can and must be a school of discipline and duty. The devotee, inasmuch as he knows that his every act must answer to God, strives to make his every act be good and according to God's will. Thus, religious consciousness informs the entire life of the man, and he is, as I have said, fertile in works. And, in the same way, national consciousness, telling citizens that certain acts of theirs must answer to the nation because then this nation can do its job, can and must *activate* in them the sense of duty and therefore the habit of discipline.

This sense of duty and habit of discipline must, above all, according to nationalism, be strongly inculcated in the citizen; that he must do his duty with the maximum discipline so that the nation might be able to do its duty. So the citizen develops a new character, thinking that he obeys an order coming from on high, and at the same time that he might collaborate in a great work, so great as to be outside every limit of his strength and vision, but which also has need of his collaboration. That is, the citizen experiences a new satisfaction, and, at the same time, feels something religious being born in him, and he begins to believe that he is obeying something divine. And he begins to act voluntarily according to this religious feeling of his national consciousness. On the day that said religiousness, o my gentlemen, exists in Italy for the many, the trains will finally depart and arrive on time; employees in municipal government and the ministries will work; the faces, words, gestures, gait, customs of Italians, instead of the present indolence, will inspire alacrity, and some of the so-called internal issues that have dragged on since the beginning of the kingdom will have finally been resolved. Because, o ladies and gentlemen, national consciousness is also a school of political chivalry.

And it is a school of sacrifice.

And this is why I have said from the start that there is a big difference between us and the perfect, bourgeois patriot, and, above all, it is egoism! Because, ultimately, nationalism is an integration between egoism, wherein the citizen asks the nation to be useful to him, and altruism, wherein the citizen does not refuse to be useful to the nation. A supreme assertion of nationalism is that the nation has a duty in and of itself, beyond every measure of force, vision, or interests, and sometimes even against the interests of the citizen, and sometimes even against the entire body of citizens. To this duty of the nation that dominates it like some divine being, with the spirit that is akin to the divine in man, the citizen must sacrifice himself and even, when necessary, unto death.

Nationalism is, in short, o gentlemen, once again, an integration! An integration between nationalism and patriotism. True patriotism, to be clear; the patriotism of our liberating fathers, not that of the perfect bourgeoisie.

Nationalism is, when all is said and done, a school of moral values, of what is commonly called virtue. We began by asserting that nationalism is a promoter of egoism and utility, the nation being a means for the economic betterment of its citizens, because that is how it is, nor has a more valid means as yet been found for the nation to procure the economic betterment of a vaster number of citizens; let us finish by asserting that nationalism is a school, the nation is an instiller of virtue. Another integration of nationalism! The integration between economic values and the moral values of a people.

Nationalism, gentlemen, is a morality.

National consciousness is the activity of this morality.

Well then, may they be inspired by this morality – the Italian state, the Italian government, the Italian ruling classes, the Italian political personnel that I have mentioned several times and in whom resides the mind and heart of the nation! Italy, then, will have a heart and a mind to perform its duty, its double duty: for the benefit of its children and for itself, as it is living in the midst of the life of the world, just as we are living in it.

In other words, our fatherland will have prosperity, wealth, and other important things, power, greatness, glory! Instead of being a subject to and parasite of another country's civilization, it will be the messenger of a new civilization to the world.

But a foundation of nationalism is the affirmation of the need for international struggle. Nations do not *acquire, they conquer!* They conquer their prosperity, their wealth, their power, their greatness, their glory, their civilization, their history in the world.

A nation, by intelligence, vigor, wholesomeness, hard work, other qualities, the very quantity of its people; by its geographical position; by the nature of its soil and the extent of its territory, by its same urgent needs; by international and historical arrangements, by one of these alone or by all these conditions together, it must possess the *initial attitudes* to become prosperous and great.

Our country possesses them!

Thus, the feeling that our fatherland will develop from the ineluctable necessity that it has, to struggle with other nations in order to conquer its prosperity and its greatness in the world; this feeling will be the best instructor of its capability to conquer its prosperity and greatness in the world. The best instructor because it is precisely that of an ineluctable necessity.

This sovereign instructor is absent in Italy today.

And perhaps this is not even the final reason that that political personnel exists today, whom I have mentioned many times. Because even today so many internal questions remain unresolved, unsolvable it appears.

But, as I have already said, the international struggle that in ordinary times is called competition, in extraordinary times is called war. A nation cannot participate with resoluteness in the international struggle without sooner or later needing to choose between peace and war.

And war is not wanted, you tell me, o gentlemen.

But I tell you, encouraging you to recall that if, in the past, among the many states into which we were divided, not a single one of them had wanted war, today perhaps we would not be a free and united nation, or we would be in a much worse condition than we are now, to be sure. But, fortunately for us, we had one, Piedmont! [Although] small, it confronted Austria. Victorious, after a few years it sent its soldiers to fight in the East. No doubt, a victorious solider who died in Chernaya, before closing his eyes, more than any other person he could have asked: "Why, for the love of God, did they send me here to die?" – He would have been unable to respond. Those he had left behind in the small, distant fatherland – his father, mother, brothers, friends, and all his contemporaries – they would have been unable to respond. Nor would the king's ministers themselves who had sent him, except one, Cavour, who knew what we know now. He knew that that small atom of an atom, that insignificant nothing that was the humble life of a soldier, it had to be sacrificed over there, far far away, in the Crimea, among the other soldiers of foreign nations, fighting against other soldiers of foreign nations, because on account of him, on account of that nobody among nobodies, that great thing that was to become Italy's freedom, gathered up by future events, could materialize finally through the eternal miracle of history.

I want to tell you, o gentlemen, that without war we would not exist.

Nor will we ever be such as our fathers saw us, with their eyes filled with hope, when they shed their own blood.

We will have poorly repaid their hope, and be-trayed our duty. The duty that we too have, to prepare a better life in a better fatherland, for those who must be born from our blood.

III. The First Nationalist Congress[8]

What I have to say will be simple and brief. I propose to put before you some things that you already know. But they will acquire a new importance if we can re-unite them under a nationalist flag.

I propose to speak to you about the conditions of our national life, pointing out to you that it will be impossible for me to speak about everything and in great detail, but only in part, and *per summa capita*, in very rapid strokes. Here are some talking points to begin with, as in a prelude to a Wagnerian melodra-ma. The important thing will be to identify the nation-alist point in each, to find for each (because you al-ready know that these conditions are not good) the means of nationalist transformation.

There is a general, fundamental, and central condition that all the particular conditions of the Ital-ian nation originate from, like a tree from its trunk. It is necessary to find this trunk in which the trouble lies, and propose the remedy according to our thought and nationalist feeling. So without further ado, let us begin.

We are a nation of emigrants, in other words we are forced to leave the fatherland and disperse throughout the world in order to have a job and to put

---

[8]Original footnote: Report presented at the first Nationalist Congress in Florence, December 3, 1910.

food on the table (this explanation in the commonest terms does not seem out of place here).

Giuseppe Bevione has in recent months published several articles on Argentina in *La Stampa*. In one article dated October 5, Bevione wrote:

> *For Argentina, Italian emigration is everything. I have said that more than two and a half million Italians have, in little less than fifty years, established themselves in the republic: that out of the six million inhabitants that Argentina has, one million are our conationals; 60 percent of our colony there is made up of farm workers. These are numbers that make one think. But there is more. Sixty-five percent of the total farm-worker population of the country is made up of Italians. A moment of reflection on this fact is enough to make one understand – for those who have not already done so – the prodigious power that is in the hands of our brothers who live in La Plata.*
>
> *The lifeblood of the country is in their hands. They are everything. Without them, Argentina would suffer famine and the shame of being unable to face its commitments with foreign countries. If the Italians of Argentina crossed their arms for one week, the life of the republic would stop as if by*

magic. If the Italian government pro-
hibited the 'golondrina' emigration[9]
for one year only, three quarters of the
harvest would rot in the fields, and Ar-
gentina would suffer more than if an
immense invasion of locusts had torn
through their fields, from Tucuman to
the Strait of Magellan, without sparing
one inch of ground.

And in a subsequent issue, on October 13, he wrote:

In Argentina, Italians do not count for
anything as a collective; and, as indi-
viduals, they must expend their energy
in an ambiance of silent but constant
hostility. It is even more pointless to
have any illusions, so fatal is it to keep
quiet about the truth and to let the de-
ception endure. The much celebrated
Italo-Argentinean brotherhood is non-
existent. There is, on the one side, our
side, submission, kindness, a love for
work, a respect for the law, deference
to the people and the things of the
country, the too acute fever to make a
fortune, which unfortunately consumes
their affection for, and recollection of,
the distant fatherland; there is, on the
other side, the Argentinean side, a
condescension, an instinctive and irre-
pressible feeling of superiority that is

---

[9]'Golondrina' emigration: i.e., a migration of swallows.

not always concealed, the frequent in-
justice and the real aversion for this
foreign element which is [ever] more
numerous, more vital, stronger, more
necessary to the republic's destinies.

And the entire article, and subsequent articles
like it, paint a picture of just what our conationals
must "put up with" in Argentina. You should read
those articles. Do you get it?! What does Italian labor
mean to Argentina? Everything. What do Italians
mean? Nothing. This is exactly the relationship that
socialism has put, and puts, the proletariat in, with respect to the bourgeoisie.

In Tunisia, not an Italian newspaper, but a
French one, *La Tunisie française*, several years ago,
on June 13, 1904, published this:

If Tunisia is prosperous today, not-
withstanding the scarce immigration
of our [French] people there, it owes
that prosperity in large part to the
cheap labor of foreign (read Italian)
farm and non-farm workers: suppress
this cheap labor, and the French capi-
tal that assures us dominion will no
longer have any good reason to come
there, and it will go away.

But to understand just how much our conationals "put up with," one needs to read in the second
issue of this year's *Bullettino dell'emigrazione* the report by our consul down there, Ugo Sabetta:

The workers are not paid in money,

but tokens that bear the mark of the company they work for and which hold currency only with the company or in its canteen. In exchange, the worker loses one percent, which ought to be the regular tax; however there have been cases in which five or even ten percent were shamelessly collected by canteen workers. It is easy to imagine the monetary gain and advantage acquired by the administration that adopts such a system of tokens: it has no need to hold large sums of money in the mines; it receives a discount on the exchange; it benefits from the tokens that are given in payment and that are lost; it obliges the miner to buy his equipment at the canteen; it often constrains him from leaving for other mines, denying him the exchange of tokens for currency.

This occurs on shores far away from where they live. The Sardinian miner is transported there, a knife is put to his throat, and he is shaken down.

The price of various victuals which should only bear the additional expense of transporting them there is instead raised a good deal higher, at certain times double, if not more; the profit increases again by passing off expired or very low-quality products for basic food items; all is weighed by

the kilo and packaged, without any op-
portunity for inspection, and the poor
miner is obliged to buy in this ex-
tremely oppressive sort of way.

You get it?! It is class exploitation, cut and dry: that of the proletariat (according to socialism) at the hands of the bourgeoisie; and there is a "compound class exploitation," or rather it is complicated by the international relations of our emigration and other countries' conquests and colonies.

And now we see yet another condition of the Italian nation. It is irredentism. I barely touch on it. When my friend Scipio Sighele publishes the *Pagine nazionaliste*[10] and when my other friend Giulio de Frenzi publishes the *Lettere dall'altra sponda*,[11] what is it that they wish to tell us? That several hundred thousand of our conationals, for instance, are destined to disappear like the last remnants of a fallen people, as if we were not of their same blood and standing as a nation beside them, already formed, thirty-five million strong. And that's enough.

But it's not enough, because we are the people of both irredentism and emigration, and in certain parts of the world, almost as if to show our status through foreshortening and symbols, we have succeeded in combining one condition with the other and in being, that is, emigrants and irredentists at the same time. In Tunisia, for example, which was al-

---

[10]*Pagine nazionaliste*: Italian for "Nationalist Pages."

[11]*Lettere dall'altra sponda*: Italian for "Letters from the Other Shore."

ready Italianized before the French conquered it, and which I already mentioned earlier with respect to our emigration. Irredentism, a circle of great powers having pressed in around us, and distant emigration: the fruit of our blood on the other side of the Ocean! As much to say, the worst of conditions. Bevione, in the articles that I have cited, recalls Japan previously as "a country like ours for the scarcity of economic resources and a superabundant population." The Japanese policy on emigration consists entirely in destroying emigration. And Bevione recalls the following words of the minister Komura:

> *Japan transformed itself from an insular empire into a continental power by consequence of a great war. Now, looking around, we see the Chinese empire of 400 million inhabitants spread out to the west of us; to the north of us, the Russian empire with 160 million inhabitants; to the east of us, the republic of the United States with 100 million. Surrounded by such heavyweight nations, the Japanese people must total at least 100 million, and therefore we must not disperse ourselves over the face of the earth, but concentrate ourselves as much as possible in one neighboring region. And in harmony with this fundamental policy the government aspired to favor emigration into Manchuria and Korea where there are ample stretches of arable land and where anywhere from*

20 to 30 million men can live. As long as emigration adopts this policy, the government will unhesitatingly favor it and protect it.

It is unnecessary to comment on that passage, with respect to the differences between the ideas that Italy has on emigration and those that Japan, an "analogous country," has.

I will briefly list other conditions. I remind you that the hospitality industry and the art of beautiful cities perpetuates in us the habit of a servile mind, and it is too much for us to have this habit at home when we are forced as well to have outside, throughout the world, the mind of an emigrant. I remind you of the invasion of foreign capital, the products of our industries battered by foreign products in our own country. Others here can recall Garda better than I can. And there are Gardas throughout Italy, where Italianity is overwhelmed by foreigners: whether more in its [economic] interest or in its dignity, we do not know.

I repeat that I can only touch on things here. With one comment I must try to suggest a hundred things to you and move on.

You and I belong to the same educated class; think over again for a moment the conditions of Italian culture, and I will read to you a quote from a recent speech by Guglielmo Ferrero:

Whoever writes the new history of Florence will be a German: whoever wants to read, not the history of a sin-

gle episode, but an entire history of the Renaissance, must resort to French, English, or German books: but what do I [an Italian] have to say about the Renaissance? Or even about the recent national Risorgimento. The latest, non-scholarly summary of this history is in English; the new historian of Cavour lives in America; the historian of Garibaldi is an Englishman; France, it appears, is preparing to give us the future historian of Mazzini. Even the latest works published in Italy about Dante are translated: one was from English, the other from German. I don't even mention Roman history: it is as if we were broadcasting to the world that we no longer have the strength to write our own history; the new Italy has hired a German to teach Roman history, in Rome.

But someone may object that these are all the conditions in which the connection between the internal and external life of the nation, between ourselves and foreigners, is evident. But we have also our internal conditions, our so-called domestic issues! Well, friends, if I wanted to speak in an exaggerated fashion, I would say that for a true nationalist, for a man who is gifted with a real national consciousness, the nation's domestic issues do not exist. But because I want to speak in a moderate fashion, I will say only that the greatest number of so-called domestic issues are false domestic issues and can always be converted into foreign issues.

For example, we have the domestic issue of the Mezzogiorno. And what is a greater domestic issue than this? All the ministers have placed it at the top of their list of government programs, and will certainly continue to do so; it is the domestic issue per antonomasia. All right-minded people of public opinion have thrown it into the face of us nationalists, so-called colonizers and imperialists, as the first domestic issue per antonomasia to be resolved! But why has none of these right-minded people of yesterday, and of the day after, thought that the Mezzogiorno issue is at least in part an emigration issue? That is, at least in part a foreign issue? Or that perhaps the entire issue of the Mezzogiorno consists in reforesting the Mezzogiorno, in a law passed by the Italian government to reforest the Mezzogiorno? No, really! At least half the Mezzogiorno issue is an emigration issue, that is, a foreign issue. And in fact, dear ladies and gentlemen, while the right-thinkers, our masters, all the political parties of the constituted and to-be-constituted order, all the ministers, were continuing to repeat: "Let us extend a hand to resolve the internal issue of the Mezzogiorno; it is time to resolve it; we do nothing if we have not first resolved the domestic issue of the Mezzogiorno!" – what happened? What happened is that the inhabitants of the Mezzogiorno, the Calabrians and the Basilicatans, for their own reasons, made a foreign issue out of what has remained a domestic issue for the entire nation, for militant high politics, for public opinion and its hundreds of newspapers. The Calabrians and Sicilians were emigrating. They took their ten centuries of misery and their patience and they crossed the Atlantic, alone having the courage to practice, for their own purposes, the politics of adventure that was denied them by national cowardice. The emigrants, gentlemen, my masters of perfect commonsense of before and after, are the precursors of imperialists, bad precursors, but precursors nonetheless.

The Mezzogiorno issue is also Sicily's issue, which because of emigration loses tens of thousands of souls per year and more, and has a desolate province. Now, I will make a supposition in order to explain my thought, but not to sketch out a program of conquest or even less a sterile lament of the past. But let us suppose that the Maghreb were Italian. Do you think that Sicily's domestic issue would be the same? I add this: do you think that it would be the same for the entire Mezzogiorno or for all of Italy? Northern Africa being under Italian rather than French dominion, do you think it would have left Sicily, the Mezzogiorno, and Italy in the same conditions that we find them in today? But the entire life of the island of Sicily, by the addition of Italian dominion on the other side of that narrow stretch of the sea, would have been shored up and brought in line with the peninsula. And the entire life of that island, the Mezzogiorno, and the peninsula would have been invigorated; and many of the so-called domestic issues that still rot in the sun today, and because of which we ourselves rot, would undoubtedly have been resolved by now. They would have been resolved after having been considered foreign issues. We would have once and for all buried our dead.

Another domestic issue is education. But, gentlemen, does the issue of education consist only in solving, or not solving, the disorders of Minerva,[12] and in equipping elementary school classrooms with benches? Or are these classrooms merely the beginning rather of a very large national effort? And then we can say how much the domestic issue has become a foreign issue, we who know how much a slave the Italian culture is (I'm recalling Ferrero) to foreign culture. We have, friends, a patrimony of masterpieces and a patrimony of moral perfections that one hundred generations of our ancestors have left to us in two thousand five hundred years of history and with three sovereignties over all other people, the sovereignty of our Greek brethren, the sovereignty of the Romans, and the sovereignty of the Renaissance. This patrimony had been like the sun to the earth, an apex of minds, a culmination of human aspirations, a mirror for the eternal human ideal, the Olympus of Gods and heroes; with it, for many centuries, we had educated our children and our youth; this had refined barbarousness, resuscitated civilization, and had been the leaven of revolutions; it had crossed the oceans together with the ships of discoverers and added new continents to the unity of humanity; it had led youthful poets, ardent and fulgurating in their blood, to their death for Italy. Eh, well, we threw them to the dogs! We threw this immense patrimony of ours, classicism, to the dogs! Let us leave it to German grammatical and lexical methods to figure it out. And now the Germanizing philologists bemoan the war that is made on classicism! But where in the world is

---

[12]Minerva: scil., the Ministry of Education.

it anymore? In other words, we have resolved a so-called domestic issue externally, but in reverse: as much to say, by subjecting our spirit to a foreign culture, rather than subjecting a foreign culture to our spirit.

Not long ago, Vincenzo Morello wrote about nationalism in the *Cronache letterarie*, and among other things he said this:

> *In the fight for existence, only the state does not have the strength, does not have the ideals, does not have the method, does not have the style. Faced with contemporary history, enemies of the state exist, but the state does not exist. Now, what is the basis of the state in Italy? Parliament. And from parliament, what thought, what word, what energy has been released over the course of so many years? What policy has ever emerged that is capable of providing for the country's interests and good fortune, I do not say for a long time, but for at minimum a decade? It is almost as if this country were a foundling, taken up by pity in a dark corner of history, none of those who had had the power to make it prosperous and happy has ever had faith in the future, and they have all sought to exploit the situation, to get by with the least amount of personal damage, and to leave people and*

things to their destiny.

And Morello added:

There was a time when it seemed that Italy too wanted, like other powers, to extend its borders into the colonial world. But after the first, foreseen, and foreseeable disasters, it engrossed itself in its own little nest, for fear of inclement weather. We are poor, the members of parliament said, and we need to become rich before allowing ourselves the luxury of a colonial life. A vicious circle that the secular members of parliamentarianism disdained to bend the arc of their minds around. Perhaps France was rich then, as it is now, when Francis I made colonial politics une affaire du roy, *when Richelieu granted titles of nobility to the bourgeoisie who went off to* exploiter *the colonies? Or England was the missus or mistress of the world when by land and by sea, warring and speculating, it had constructed in two centuries of uninterrupted battle its colonial empire? Or are the riches of either nation not the consequence of all those efforts and all those struggles? We were witnesses, one could say, of the creation of German colonial politics. The victors of Sedan arrived late to the banquet: the good*

> *places were all occupied. And without*
> *growing discouraged, they acted and*
> *occupied those that remained, even*
> *below the Tropics.*

Well, these sad and just notes by Vincenzo
Morello are enough to show how the clearly domestic
issue of our parliamentarianism, which is our entire
political world, is a chronicle of suppressed external
acts. Not long ago, Scipio Sighele wrote the following
in *La Stampa:*

> *I believe that everyone will agree in*
> *recognizing that he who governs Italy*
> *today is a patriot. Well, this patriot*
> *who goes by the illustrious name of*
> *Luigi Luzzatti has summarized his po-*
> *litical credo in two phrases: Italians*
> *who love the fatherland must stop be-*
> *ing interested in foreign policy; they*
> *must maintain the peace even at the*
> *cost of every baseness.*

Well, gentlemen, the patriot Luigi Luzzatti,
that flower of our parliamentarianism, is unfortunately a domestic problem of ours. But you do all understand that the politics of this domestic problem
would be the suicide of Italy in the world, don't you?

But we digress.

We must start from the recognition of this
principle: there are proletarian nations, just as there
are proletarian classes; nations, that is, whose conditions of life are disadvantageously subjected to those
of other nations, just like classes. On that premise, na-

tionalism must first and foremost work hard at this first truth: Italy is materially and morally a proletarian nation. And it is proletarian in the period before the reconquest, that is, in the preorganic period of blindness and vital debility. Subjected to other nations and debile, not in popular forces, but in national ones. Precisely as the proletariat was before socialism approached it.

The workers' muscles were as strong as today, but what will did the workers have to rise up? They were blind to their condition. Now, what happened when socialism spoke the first word to the proletariat? The proletariat woke up, had a first glimpse of its condition, saw the possibility of changing it, conceived the first plan of changing it. And socialism pulled it along; pushed it to fight; formed in the struggle its union, its consciousness, its strength, its own arms, its new right, its will to succeed, its pride to overcome; freed it; compelled it to dictate its class law to other classes, to the nation, to nations.

Well, friends, nationalism must do something similar for the Italian nation. It must, to make a poor comparison, be our national socialism. That is, just as socialism taught the proletariat the value of the class struggle, so must we teach Italy the value of the international class struggle.

But the international class struggle is war?

Well, let it be war! And let nationalism rouse in Italy the will for victorious war.

It is superfluous to point out that our war is not a running to arms, and that our victorious war is not a poetic or prophetic ingenuity, but a moral order. What we are proposing in short is a "method of national redemption"; and, with an extremely recapitulatory and concentrated expression, we call it the "necessity of war." War is the supreme act, but to assert it as the necessity of war involves recognizing the necessity of preparing for war and preparing oneself for war; that is, it involves a technical method and a moral method. A method of national discipline. A method to create the formidable and ineluctable reason for the necessity of national discipline. A method to create the inexorable necessity of a return to the feeling of duty. Nationalists take it to heart that schools and railroads do their duty. A method to restore credit primarily to virtue and to the exercise of virtue (the methods of Japan, poor like us) which the bourgeoisie and their public opinion and their commonsense and ruling classes and politicians, or parliamentarianism, as Vincenzo Morello would say, put off to one side with respect to the life of the Italian nation. A method finally to renew a pact of familial solidarity among classes of the Italian nation. A method to prove the necessity and usefulness of this pact. For years and years, it was preached to Italian workers by socialism, our master and our adversary, that it was in their best interest to unite themselves with the workers from Cochin China and Paraguay and to break every solidarity with their bosses and the Italian nation. It must be pounded into the heads of the workers that they have a major interest in maintaining strong ties with their bosses and above all with their nation; and in sending to the devil any solidarity with their companions of Paraguay and Cochin

China.

In summary, since the time it was founded on freedom and unity, Italy has lost two wars and it has not resolved the question of the Mezzogiorno. In the politics of alliances it has succeeded in becoming the enemy of its allies and the friend of its allies' enemies, without any credit with either. It has not even suspected that emigration could be directed towards a national purpose, and it has by now worn down all its institutions and exhausted all its parties.

As much to say, the result of our foreign policy and domestic policy is bad.

What are the reasons? There is a need to work at a general revision. Nationalism proposes this work. There is a need to change the system, to find a better system of men and things. Nationalism wants to find it. This is its reason for being.

Part II
Militant Politics

IV. Democratic Aristocracy and Oligarchic Democracy

Experience from the most recent political elections in October and November 1913 teaches, to those who see clearly, that among the many parties we have, the one that calls itself the grand old Liberal Party, if it wants to continue leading the political life of the nation, will need to transform itself into a grand new nationalist party, while adopting the doctrine, thought, and method of struggle from that nationalism that has recently been its vanguard.

Only then will it be able to stand up to its natural antagonist which is the Socialist Party.

The present historical reality sees before it two political positions: that of the Socialist Party, and that of the Nationalist Party.

Whoever, for example, sees the usual Liberal Party as between two opposite extremes, the socialists and clericals, and makes his future triumph depend on them, and the health of the fatherland consequently, by keeping equidistant from both, is someone who does not see clearly, probably because of an old sectarian mindset. The opposites here, if anything, are the clericals and the Masonics. But beyond that, the historical reality involves the two major opposing parties: the Socialist Party and the Nationalist Party.

The duty of the latter must be to work for domestic pacification, with the goal of augmenting the nation's wealth and power, as a means to reaching the ultimate national aim whose realization resides in world conflict. Now, by working towards that, the Nationalist Party will come to find itself antagonistically at odds with socialism which is internationally pacifistic as a result of the domestic class struggle.

But in the contemporary historical reality there are other parties. They are all those parties that lie somewhere between socialism and old-style liberalism, which call themselves democratic and which can be considered unified in one large democratic party because of their common essence.

With respect to which, how will the Nationalist Party that we need to form determine whether it has the fatherland at heart?

To respond to this question we need to point out the difference that exists between two words that commonly have the same meaning. The two words are adversary and enemy. Socialism is the adversary, the antagonist, as we have said; and democracy, not what would be democracy according to its theoretical definitions, which amount to less than nothing in terms of political action, but the democratic reality operating in Italy today – that is the enemy.

The case against democracy is well-known even in Italy. But only in Rome, during the elections, did I clearly see to the bottom of it. We must think back on the democracy of Roman princes. We must think of the two Roman princes, Don Leone Caetani

and Don Scipione Borghese, who launched their electoral campaign based on their democracy. But first, to
act the proper gentleman, I must preface it with this:
that if I talk about Roman princes, it is not intended to
nurture a special rancor towards those illustrious electoral victims of ours, nor to attribute what they say
and do merely to their own personal fault; the blindness of the times is in them and they do not see or
know what they do. But I mention them precisely because as electoral fortunes would have it, in the capital city they were singled out as a problem that is
common to all the classes of the old aristocracy, the
wealthy bourgeoisie, the working class, the educated
class. I take them for what they were at a solemn moment in time: prototypes and a memorable example.
And I have no intention of speaking against them and
others like them, but rather to speak for them and for
others like them, in order to enlighten them. With that
out of the way, let's return to our story. One evening,
then, in Rome, I went to a meeting that was taking
place in I don't remember what piazza. On a stand beneath a doorway the Prince Caetani was speaking, but
the crowd of adversaries was raising a din to make
him stop. In the obscurity of the approaching night, I
saw the long arms of the prince gesticulating over the
noisy crowd, while he continued obstinately to vocif-
erate. I grasped only one word, that of his program:
democracy. Then, suddenly, I saw clearly, as we used
to say, into heart of contemporary democracy.

In a few words, here is the law, nor can it be
stated any more completely or exactly: society is organized just as it is for the defense and preservation
of established interests, and for the propulsion and de-

velopment of interests to be established. There are two functions, preservation and development, which can then be reduced to one, in that preservation, if what is intended is that true one which must be and is, in other words, a living and organic preservation and not that of the greedy who grasp at and hide treasures – preservation, I repeat, for the very reasons of its organic life, like every form of organic life that carries within itself all the propulsions of its development and is, as much to say, by natural necessity, progressive. Which is no longer understood in our times when everyone, in one way or another, proclaims the progressive function of society – liberals, democrats, radicals, not to mention socialists, republicans, and anarchists – and not one among them is found who is not ashamed, with a feeling of shame for our times, to affirm the social conservative function which is, at the very least, equally necessary, licit, and honest. However, getting back to the topic at hand, we must say that the more defense that established interests need for their preservation, the more established they are over a long period of time, because their justice is always less manifest; not only that, but their conditioning is also out of step with the times, and therefore their solidarity is always weaker. But among all the long-established interests, first and foremost are those of aristocratic patrimonies and, so as not to lose sight of our champions who serve us so well, those of a latifundiary nature among the Roman princes of papal origin. Maximal therefore is the effort that society, the state, all of us, must make to defend them. Well, while this effort is being made, what are our many noble gentlemen doing in the meanwhile – what are our Roman princes doing, for goodness sake? We need to distinguish between their private life and their public life. In their private life, the noble gentlemen, the Roman princes, act as latifundistas, but in their public life they stump for democracy. In their private life, our excellent Roman champions do nothing to modernize their just possession of latifundia, modernizing their management of them, but in their public life they act as the candidates of democratic parties who have the future, the progress, and the advancement of humanity in their programs by definition. In their private life, they do nothing to reduce their dependence on the state, like today, for the preservation of their interests, but in their public life they do all they can to lead the state towards democratic novelties which ought to make that defense of their interests increasingly more difficult. In their private life and in the firmness of their interests, they are ultimately reactionaries, but in their public life and in their sympathy with social altruism they are so democratic that in order to provide for the future of the proletariat and the "less privileged classes" in general they attempt to lend a helping hand to socialism. During the electoral campaign, the *Idea nazionale* published letters by noblemen who knew *de visu* of the estates held by Prince Borghese and which, inasmuch as they reported, they could prove with documents. There is in Rome, as the readers know, an institute of culture for opening schools in the Agro. Here is how the democratic prince, ennobler of the national and international proletariat, practices the ennoblement of *his* proletariat.

In the Pantano estate, the buildings
for schools were not and are not pro-

vided by the prince, but rather by the tenants, the affluent Gibelli. At Torre-nova, the buildings were sufficient as long as the tenant furnished them, but as soon as they are furnished by the prince, they are inadequate, indecent, and fetid. Thus, indeed, or with other adjectives equally wanting in praise, is the official report of the committee for schools expressed with regards to them. The prince's estate contributed to the awards ceremony! Yes, but by sending by way of gift from Rome ten or twelve shiny metal watches. And that's it. The prince has never visited the schools.

And now, after the joys of moral uplift, the joys of economic uplift.

In Pantano, there are about 50 fami-lies of farmhands, they are nomads, *they work under a foreman, they still live in* shanties! *The blessed cholera of 1911 advised the destruction of that sad village; but the village was rebuilt naturally with shanties and small tem-porary housing made of* Eternit.[13] *That is to say, things returned to the way they were. Same wages, same mis-eries, same brutification. This state of things, if it is not expressly desired by*

---

[13]Eternit: the brand name for a composite of cement-asbestos used for some items of construction, or manufacturing, like corrugated roofing sheets, aqueduct pipes, etc.

the proprietor, is tolerated.

The farmers depend, it is true, on the tenant, who runs their affairs, but unfortunately the reclamation and sanitation laws do not adequately protect the life of the workers, who have neither a labor contract nor worker's compensation, nor the most elemental standards of hygiene that guarantee humane lodging, healthy food, or potable water. In Pantano, until two years ago, the farmers drank water from a ditch! The fountain with potable water was located more then two kilometers away from the shanty village, and the winter roads were quagmires!

Of course, the latifundista could have imposed on the tenant to provide houses, nourishing food, rules of civilized life, assistance to the workers who in any case assured him of payment of the rent. The fact is that the Prince Borghese, however brilliant an orator and expert in agriculture he might be, does not himself bother with agriculture per se, he does not live in the country. He has his agents who perhaps inform him poorly; but if he had had a humanitarian spirit and the experience of an agriculturalist, he would have visited his lands more of-

ten and provided for them.

As for the Prince Borghese's other estate, Torrenova, it is the same. Ocular witnesses speak about it in the *Idea nazionale:*

> *I remember having seen, the following year as well, a smoky and putrescent bedlam in the old farmhouse where the* indigents *slept on filthy sacks spread out on the bare ground. It was evening and the air was unbreathable, thick, blinding with the smoke from the hearths where the destitute cooked polenta. Torrenova is ten kilometers from Rome and subject to reclamation! Even in Torrenova, new lodgings were insufficient for the population, and the greedy tenant treated the men worse than animals. But the proprietor prince, why did he allow it? Perhaps he didn't know about it? And if that's the case, he does not know what happens in his own backyard! A sign that he seldom visits the country, his country estate! If he knew, he would have made the tenant treat the workers humanely. For example, a proprietor of houses that wants to be respected does not rent his house to people... who treat it poorly! The sight of the shanties in Pantano and the destitution in Torrenova produce a feeling of disgust and indignation in whoever*

sees it.

Readers can imagine the effort that society, that the state, that all of us must make so that the Roman princes can, in this day and age, conserve such patrimonies that hearken back to a regime of such medieval iniquity! Well, meanwhile what are the Roman princes doing, how do they repay society, and the state, all of us, for the effort we make for them? They repay us in this way. They ought, if they did not possess the blindness of the century, they ought to do everything in their power to make the medieval iniquity disappear from their lands, and in public they should remain quiet and not talk. On the contrary, they do nothing to make the iniquity disappear from their lands, they keep *their* people on the latifundia under a regime of medieval iniquity, but in public they act like friends of the people, subscribe to political parties that act like friends of the people, and run as the candidates of parties that are friends of the people. In other words, they are not friends of *their* people, which would cost them something, but they are friends of *others'* people, which costs them nothing, but costs the state and others something. In other words, concluding finally, they contribute by making it more difficult for the work of social defense and social preservation which are necessary for everyone, including the nation, but which the people above all have an extreme need for. The latter make it harder and more difficult by rushing into the arms of those who menace them more, because they have an idea of the second function of the social institution, the function of renewal, which is in no way, shape, or form different from the idea of subversion.

Such is the democracy of our aristocratic lords, which for antonomasia we have agreed to call the democracy of Roman princes.

And yet the mental blindness of the majority is so great that it is not noticed that such democracy is nothing more than a position of double personal convenience: personal convenience in private to do what suits them, personal convenience in public to espouse a policy that is in line with the spirit of the times.

It is not noticed that such democracy is nothing more than an attitude of double personal interest: private personal interest, public personal interest.

The nature of contemporary democracy is all there: in being content with a political statement that is not in line with, but often antagonistically opposed to, the personal, economic, and voluntary reality of the individual.

And the possibility of deception in which democracy keeps the public: it is all there: in its benefiting from an immoral, hypocritical, too-convenient distinction between private life and public life, for which [reason] people no longer see the necessary nexus between the personal reality of the man which is the basis of every other reality and his political statement which, separated from that basis, is either meaningless talk or talk with ulterior motives.

To maintain that deception about the suppression of the so-called nexus is a matter of life or death for contemporary democracy.

In Rome, during the elections, it was very instructive to see in what way the democratic newspapers supported the candidature of democratic princes. They supported them, saying that the princes were democratic and that their adversaries were clerico-nationalists. Those newspapers knew about the latifundia of the Agro better than we did, but denied it, or did not care. The princes were democratic, they were candidates of democracy, and the democratic newspapers supported them.

The truth is that the position of our democratic aristocracy and the position of the democratic newspapers are the same. It is the same position of political exposition that has nothing in common with the reality of its expositor. With the difference that the solid, concrete reality of the democratic aristocracy is a landed property of feudal origins, while the solid, concrete reality of the democratic newspapers is a super modern joint-stock company.

Around the time of the Libyan War, two democratic newspapers belonging to the same company, one in Rome, *Il Messaggero*, and one in Milan, *Il Secolo*, were of the opposite opinion; the Roman one, as readers know, was pro-Libyan, the Milanese one was anti-Libyan. Very good, the ingenuous think, this is how democracy understands the freedom of conscience of its servants. But the truth is otherwise. It is the robust indifference of the administrations, of the joint-stock companies, of the democratic newspapers, for any sort of public opinion whatsoever, even of such high national importance as the Libyan War. When one wants to launch a democratic newspaper, one finds a director who has a certain democratic past, and this is easy to do because democracy spans from any sort of liberalism to reformist socialism, with a tendency toward possible alliances even with revolutionaries. So a director already active in the so-called democratic ranks is selected then, to whom is added an editorial staff with some reformist socialists and some transigent republicans, or intransigent, depending, in addition to the corpus of journalists who are predominantly revolutionary socialists; this excellent group is allowed to develop the democratic program (in good faith, gentlemen, in good faith, which is less dishonest, but so much more comical!), and meanwhile the administration, the *ad hoc* man, from whose views (which are not at all political, but only financial) the democratic newspaper emerges, gives, or at least proposes to give, substantial dividends to the shareholders of the company whose members, of course, include no small number of the most perfect type of bourgeois boor who does everything in his power in life to ensure a good return on his investment, and nothing to possess a sustainable political opinion.

In one of the most illustrious cities of Italy there exists a democratic newspaper that serves as a government organ for the region, and as an organ of liberal associations for the city; it supported candidates from both groups in prior elections, plus its own system of opposite candidatures: a socialist candidature in one place and a clerical one in another; conformant with a unity, we have no doubt, of sound administrative direction, not to mention a variety of independent political editorial opinions fluctuating under that directorial one which is naturally democratic. It was, we believe, in all of Italy the only newspaper that in past elections succeeded in earning the distinction of being beaten twice, in two different cities and on two antagonistic programs: backing the pro-government candidates in its city, and backing the Campanozzian[14] revolution in Rome. Now this incomparable model of democratic newspapers had among its editors a revolutionary socialist, who was also a syndicalist, a petroleur, a bombardier, and the like. He was put forward as a candidate, and in order to be a free citizen he left the newspaper that had, as we mentioned earlier, its own candidate in the same constituency. It is superfluous to add that for the entire electoral period the newspaper and its ex-editor tore into each other, not stopping short of immorality. On the very morning of October 26, the newspaper revealed that after all this time the ex-editor had continued to visit the administration requesting loans, and this seemed like a shameless immorality to it. In the evening, the ex-editor lost. When lo and behold, several days later, the newspaper announces that, never having had a good reason to disesteem him, it offered him his post back, and thus the revolutionary returned to the democratic newspaper. But that wasn't the end of it. It became known that this came about because of the good offices of a friend. Eh, well, guess who it was, o gentlemen? The losing journalist's victorious adversary, a man with a good heart and in part a radical. The illustrious city, stupefied, still wonders what the paper's political opinions are, into which it can have the naïvety even of inserting a bit of its soul and well-being; what are they for the multifarious follow-

---

[14]Campanozzian: in reference to Antonino Campanozzi, lawyer, journalist, socialist, and member of Parliament.

ers of diverse democracy.

What are they?

We have already seen it: they are business positions. It is patently clear by now that businessmen,
great industrialists, great builders, bankers, the so-
called greats, the men of enterprise, the *equites ro-
mani* of the Third Italy, that is, the commendatores of
anonymous societies, have a marked inclination for
democracy. It is like this in France, and it is like this
also in Italy. Why? For the love of democracy perhaps? Not in your wildest dreams. Why then? For the
benefit they gain by appearing democratic, by moving
in a certain atmosphere of democratic favor. Because
democracy, for Puritanism, for Popularism, for socialism, above all for envy, avidity, and hypocrisy, would
not be averse to casting the producers of wealth in a
bad light, let us say socially, and for that reason they
seek to ingratiate themselves with it and keep their
mouths shut. They succeed in pocketing their salaries.
In the same aristocrats, from whom we have agreed to
elect Roman princes as champions, and in the rich
bourgeois who make a pretense of being democrats –
the same thing happens: even in them, in advance of
the instinct of ambition, a deeper instinct is at work,
the instinct of self-preservation. The subconscious-
ness warns them that under the current circumstances,
a democratic display is the best protection for them
against letting go of their wealth, their titles, their refined indulgence, their idleness. Then the democratic
display also provides a career path, as we say, to their
ambition. And so on and so forth for the new producers of wealth, businessmen, industrialists, builders,

and finally the new producers of modern liquid wealth, who replace the heirs of the old, original, landed wealth or at least the feudal model. At the price of a democratic newspaper they intend to buy a certain exemption from work and production and, what is more, assisted by the opportunism of the already puritanical democracy, they acquire a greater freedom of movement and a greater boldness in their affairs; they have, when they want it and for those who want it, the means, through the democratic newspaper which is in their pay, to exert pressure, for example, on the state by means of contracts, commissions, and supplies. So this creator of the raw material of national greatness, the producer of wealth, is often corrupt and itself corrupts through the agency of democracy made most accommodating and most complacent after having begun as the scourge of every corruption. Democracy develops bad instincts that are at the root of its Puritanism, greed, and envy, and derives from it a preponderant dynamic of voracity. The businessman profits by it.

In past elections we had edifying examples: in some Italian cities we saw newspapers strongly pressured by yards that furnished the state with shells and cannons to support socialist candidates. Militarism and anti-Militarism in lockstep? Of course. The industrial-democratic complex offers them a point of combination for both their benefit. I remember a constituency in Tuscany where the socialist candidate was supported by nearly all the landowners. One of them, a factory owner, a noble, after my having asked him why he backed a socialist, responded to me: "Try to understand me! I have a hand in that constituency.

Previously our candidate was one of the more relent-
less socialists, but then he saw the light and became
domesticated. You understand! The support we give
him, it is an insurance premium." And when I said to
him: "But the country? Why aren't you thinking
about the good of the country?" And the nobleman
said to me: "And why should I think about it? Isn't
that the government's job? Besides, the king does the
same thing in the capital. I hear that he influences
people to vote for Leonida Bissolati." Even the
crown? With all due respect to the nobleman, let's
leave the crown out of it. But the nobleman's words
are correct: democracy is the insurance policy that is
paid in public for one's private use.

Thus far we have passed under review various
incarnations of contemporary democracy: the democracy of aristocrats, with its two sides, its instinct for
self-preservation and its electoral instinct; the democracy of newspapers and the democracy of businessmen; industrial democracy.

To which we ought to add the great infernal
machine of contemporary democracy: Masonic
democracy.

But recently this machine has been too much
dismantled, piece by piece; it has been shown to function too much in Masonic secrecy and in bloc, under
the tutelage of universal democracy and its high
ideals. Men from every political party have emerged,
of which socialists like Enrico Ferri who evolved toward the bourgeoisie from which they came, socialists ripe for government, like Leonida Bissolati, fully-
baked reformists, republicans who on account of

Libya blew up the hovel of their republic, radicals who have their people in the ministry, democrats (municipal careerists), constitutionalists (because of the king, who made them commendatores), all of whom, between October 26 and November 2, we saw converge to enter the lists in support of the candidacy of the anti-Libyan revolutionary socialist Antonino Campanozzi. Who made them bend? The occult power of the Freemasons. Who held them together again? The Masonic link. When every other link had been broken, when every other dependency had ended, the Masonic link remained, the occult power of the Freemasonry remained. In the depths of contemporary democracy, beneath all democratic combinations, beneath all the party lines of thought, lies the occult Masonic power, a power of the most tenacious oligarchy wrapped in the mystical ephod of universal principles. From this subterranean oligarchic reality, through the opportunism of [Masonic] brethren and the greed of municipal blocs, Freemasonry rises to its public democratic display.

In summary, and to conclude, Masonic democracy, aristocratic democracy, electoral democracy, the democracy of newspapers, the democracy of businessmen and other workers in the capital, is like this! All contemporary democracy has a criminal nature. Its criminality consists in what we have brought to light, in its having a political display of altruistic, popular, proletarian, socialist, humanitarian, progressive and civil character, as a cover up and to promote its true nature which is made up of selfishness and egotistical exploitation.

Such is democracy in the present historical period: a democracy of exploitation, of individual parasitism.

As we said at the outset, the present historical period puts two antagonistic positions before us: the socialist position of proletarian and internationalist interests, and the nationalist position of the interests of all classes and the nation. But democracy lands somewhere between these two and muddles everything up, even the conflict.

And for this reason democracy is the common enemy of the two adversaries, socialism and the nation.

Because in public life the adversaries, while fighting each other, collaborate and create what is new for the future, while the enemy is what wears down forces, exploits forces, squanders the present and destroys the future.

V. Liberals and Nationalists[15]

The counting of the ballot boxes had not yet finished in past elections and already the Liberal Party, rather bruised, summoned its ranks and put forward the call to "reorganize itself." First it was the pure, abstinent *condottiere* of the forward sentinels of the Liberal Party, Giovanni Borelli, to raise his vehement voice in *Il Resto del Carlino* of Bologna.

What happened several days later, you know, o gentlemen. By means of the Roman newspaper which is an exponent of the serious political consciousness of the Hon. Sonnino, *Il Giornale d'Italia*, by means of an acephalous leader of the Catholic Association, the Count Gentiloni, by means of clerics, by means of anti-clerical Freemasons, the clamor of pact signatories was let loose on the public, and even before Montecitorio had reopened, Parliament returned to troubling Italy. That was the first act of the new legislature. It was known that, give or take one candidate's name, or ten, or more than two hundred and perhaps even more than three hundred, from among those who won and those who lost, each had thought during the campaign about the particular interests of his constituency and had done what had seemed most practical to him in his own way, without concern for anything else. Without concern for the political morality, and let's say even the human

---

[15]Original footnote: From a discourse given in Venice, Genoa, Turin, Naples, etc. in December 1913.

morality, of his election. And I point this out, not so
much for the fact itself, but because also on that occasion those who know them found the liberals as they
had left them: members of a party that offered them
nothing to fight with anymore, neither solid ground,
nor arms, nor spirit; nor the reality, that is, of interests
and positions, nor the reality of doctrine, nor the reality of feelings, nothing; for which, in order even to
win, they resorted to whatever means came to hand.
Men of decadence, extreme decadence, not so much
in themselves and their qualities, but rather because it
is always about decadence and extreme decadence for
the average human being when the spirit of life, of
whatever life, or politics, or religion, or morality in
general, and in whatever way you choose, is poor in
the ambient and circulating atmosphere. We know of
liberal candidates whose entire electoral campaign
was spent in continual agreement of mutual support
with socialist candidates of adjacent constituencies
who had their own liberal candidate even. This is the
typical case, and the exception. But under the exception lies the rule, in the spirit of the liberal doctrine
that leaves its men exposed. And these men, having a
certain ambition, and not exceeding without demerit
or merit of their own the average person, and wanting
to play a part in public life, do what they can.

Several months before the elections, we were
speaking with a liberal deputy of considerable esteem,
a serious, studious, and fine person in all respects,
who said to us: "we need to 'reorganize' the Liberal
Party, but we lack men." You said that right, we
thought to ourselves. But now, if we imagine that
they are speaking about doctrines first and men sec-

ond, we hear the same thing repeated first by this person and then by that person: that the doctrines would seem to be lacking in men, and the men lacking in doctrine, and they would both be right. You have heard the speech made to the house recently by one of the esteemed leaders of liberalism, a distinguished politician, the Hon. Salandra, a man of fervent patriotic feeling; but tell me whether it was not another display of a worn-out doctrine! Freedom, sovereignty of the state, meridional matters, and patriotism understood as idealism, but not much more.

But liberals always declare, and before and immediately after elections, that they need to "reorganize" their party, and nothing more; they do not think of anything more profound. When the elections go poorly, liberals, monarchists, those of the so-called party of order in short, they always end their lamentations with the same accusation against the electorate, their electorate, which "has abandoned the ballot boxes for indolence," while the socialist's electorate have flocked to the ballot boxes "united." They do not suspect, the liberals, the monarchists and the like, that the cause of their electorate's indolence could reside in something other than their electorate's indolence; they have forgotten the Latin motto: *spiritus inter alit*, and the Italian translation of this expression is this: there is either a soul within, or it dies.

It is not my intention to paint a complete picture here of the spectacle that liberalism makes of itself; my intention rather is to research the causes of it.

Why has liberalism come into its present decadence?

Because, I immediately respond, it was a very poor combatant against socialism. A combatant – allow me the sincerity which alone is useful – without courage and without intelligence.

This is the raw and naked truth.

When the Socialist Party appeared on the political scene, the liberals, if they wanted to continue being the effective leaders of national life, would have immediately had to see their enemy as not merely an annoyance to keep at bay, but an antagonistic enemy to fight bitterly and relentlessly against.

Why, you ask me, did the Socialist Party step forward in the first place and declare war on the bourgeoisie in the name of the proletariat?

And why not?

Why should liberalism have forgotten that it originated with the bourgeoisie, that it was a conception, a creation, a historical and political state of the bourgeoisie since its first rise to power, since the French Revolution? And, consequently, why should it not have been the defender of the bourgeoisie? It was socialism, according to historical conditions, that had given it substance and dynamics – was it or was it not a new force that attempted to expropriate the bourgeoisie economically and dispossess them politically? And that being the case, gentlemen, why should another force not have come in its way, fighting for bourgeois property and supremacy over the bourgeoisie? But an energetic force, it must be said, steadfast, courageous and intelligent, understanding its right to stay the course, just as the enemy understood its right to conquer?

This defense of the bourgeoisie, however, should have been the liberals' minor program only, and their major program should have been something else altogether. Liberalism should have proceeded far and beyond the defense of the bourgeoisie. It should have been able to move forward, with more courage and even more intelligence, to confront socialism, not so much because socialism was striking at the bourgeoisie, but because by striking at the bourgeoisie it was striking at the nation. Then, indeed, Italian liberalism would have assumed its great historical position.

But in order to do this, liberalism should have had a consciousness that was full and energetic, steadfast, courageous, and intelligent – about something that was not insignificant: the existing, organic union between the bourgeoisie and the nation, the union of one bodily organ to another that had a ruling function. And it should have had a consciousness resolved for any action just to prove in broad daylight that it was the political agent, the party, of that ruling class. And then, while it reunited the organ to the body, the bourgeoisie to the nation, the partial interests of the bourgeoisie to the total interests of the nation – while, in other words, it was subordinating this to that, as is done with a part to the whole – liberalism would have come to conceive in itself a new national soul that would have given it the strength to take what we have called its great historical position and confront the socialist party's two positions which were hostile to the nation and which was the class struggle within, and the international class struggle without.

Instead, in opposition to the class struggle, what did the Liberal Party, the liberal government, the liberal state do?

They all exhausted themselves in a declaration, in the declaration, that is, of the freedom to strike and to work. And they really could have done something more. Something more than a like policy which is passive, static, inert, a simple statement that the right of intervention is denied. They could have practiced a policy that is not a declaration, but an action, not a declaration, but something of substance. Of national substance pitted against socialist content. The socialist content was economical then? Was it, in short, the class struggle for a different distribution of wealth? And liberalism should have filled the void that had been made over time in its program, with an entirely new supply of economic content, of this economic content: the cooperation of the classes for a greater production of national wealth. Which is action pitted against action, goal against goal, result against result, and not according to the excogitations of men and the deliberations of parties, but according to precise indications and the insuppressible necessity of the historical period that it was going through! Instead, liberalism did nothing at all with all that. It merely enacted a reform policy, a policy of social assistance, and often that was fine, often that was the right thing to do; but this policy was only what it conceded to socialism through its organic weakness, what in its timidity it conceded to socialism, not by constructive initiative. In order to construct, it should have been, for example, the author of an entire legislation aimed at favoring an increase in the production of wealth, as we were saying, the author of an entire industrial and commercial legislation, o gentlemen. But political liberalism, through a kind of inertia, through an incapacity to develop, and for other reasons, has always kept its distance from industries and from commerce and their fortunes; it did not inspire a government, and even less the state, to favor them. It may even have inspired one to damage them. To be sure, political liberalism has always remained political in a small and mean way, nothing more; it has never understood that it had political adversaries of extremely strong economic substance around it. It contented itself by remaining window dressing where others had a body.

And now, coming around to the second, anti-nationalist position of socialism, to its internationalism, we ask ourselves: What should have been the historical task of Italian liberals? What was their historical task in response to the socialist conception of all the workers of the world united in one large organic body that, consequently, was going to abolish the old national unities? What was the liberals' task?

Alas! We are now at the most serious point in this examination of our liberalism. Recently, Prof. Alfredo Rocco of the University of Padua wrote the following in *La Tribuna*:

> *After 1870, the country having been unified by this time, it seemed that the national task of Italy had been completed. The opinion that unification*

*was a goal in itself was widely circu-
lated, more as a feeling than as a consciousness. A part of the old party of
action remained fighting, it is true, for
the national idea, but only because it
did not consider the fatherland completely unified. Outside this minority,
all the other currents of political parties turned elsewhere. The populist
parties, on the example of foreign
democracies, turned towards the ideal
of social justice, then incarnated by
the* International. *The old party of action, whose program, with the attain-
ment of unification, had been emptied
of content, became a purely parliamentary party with no other preoccu-
pation than to attain power... In truth,
the old left was, after 1870, a simple
phenomenon of* survival: *its specific
function had ceased, and it continued
to exist by force of habit and by tradition. The old right remained. It, which
had been the party of precaution and
prudent audacity during the heroic period, and which had operated magnifi-
cently in this way as long as Cavour
was leading it, and mediocrely when
the great statesman had disappeared,
had also lost its foothold with the ful-
fillment of unification. And, on a par
with the other parties, it did not know
how to transform itself. It too, like the
left, saw nothing after the fulfilled uni-*

fication.

These remarks by Prof. Rocco are correct. After which, coming to the transformation accomplished on March 18, 1876, of the two old parties of the right and left in the new, so-called "great Liberal Party," the writer adds:

> *But, alas! if the old right and the old left, after 1870, had seen their programs devoid of any ideal content, and if they had made a mistake, the two of them, in believing that with the fulfillment of Italian unification the task of Italy was complete, there is no need to think that the new Liberal Party was in any better condition. Divided by personal rivalries and memories of old political dissensions, threatened by the progress of socialism, it too did not have, one might say, a program, and existed, one might say, almost exclusively for its electoral interests. There was, it is true, the parenthesis, indeed there were Crispian parentheses. But the Crispi phenomenon constituted the affirmation of an individual political genius, not the action of a party. Yes, Crispi really did have a great political ideal; he understood that Italy could not have been created simply for the sake of creating it; but that unification had to be the starting point of a great work of renewal, in order to obtain*

*economic and moral greatness inter-
nally, and affirmation of the Italian
nation's place in the world externally.*

This is true. Just as internally the necessary
historical reaction against the class struggle, which
socialism had proclaimed, was missing, so too with
the external life of the nation, that reaction against the
internationalism that socialism had put on an economic footing was missing.

Parallel to this grandiose event, to this internationalism, to this true and proper class imperialism of
the last class to come to power, parallel and related,
dependent on the same causes – an even more
grandiose event was happening in the world. It was
the European colonialism that was conquering and
transforming Africa and Asia. On such a topic, Italian
liberals, the majority party of the government and nation, that is, remained in that same state of blindness
that the rest of the common people of Italy did, the
plebs of universitarian culture and popular analpha-
betism. And they did not snap out of it, neither
through Francesco Crispi, as Rocco duly noted, nor
afterward. Francesco Crispi was either an adversary
or, with very few individual exceptions, he was reluctantly followed, and when he fell out of power that
dawn of greatness of the Third Italy was swept away
by the horrible conspiracy. And afterwards it persist-
ed in the old optimistic ideas about emigration,
which, as you know, ladies and gentlemen, is, on the
contrary, the way in which those nations that have
such an impoverished proletariat practice great, modern colonialism – so as to be considered poor and

working class people themselves. It is the way of colonizing people before their redemption on what will be the field of their effort and future power. But Italy from its natural field of the Mediterranean and the continents that enclose it, followed the flight of its children to distant America for the longest time; and, not realizing that by crossing over the ocean they had to cut themselves off from her, as she from them, it judged their fortune optimal and ideal. And it celebrated their flight and celebrated the so-called free colonies, especially Argentina, its favorite, and having no other reason to celebrate itself, it celebrated the sweat of the brow that those many hundreds of thousands of its Basilicatans, Calabrians, and Venetians exuded in order to till the lands and build the roads in the *caipira fazenda* and the *estancia gaucha,* both vassals of the gold possessed by the two capitalistic nations of Europe, England and France.

Well then, such blindness that for many years belonged to all of Italy, also belonged to its major national party and government, namely the liberals. On such a score they were blind, deaf, and mute.

And when, finally, the great proletariat moves, others and not them, not them, not the liberals, will move it. The Tripoli undertaking will be accomplished by an eclectic minister, and others, not the liberals, others will move public opinion.

In short, in the period that goes from Adwa to Tripoli, in a part of the Italian soul, as you know, ladies and gentlemen, a new consciousness will form, or better yet there will be a return to the concept of good old common sense, that the nation in its internal life is not an end in itself, but that its ends are external, in the world. It will return to recognize and reaffirm the subordination of domestic politics to foreign policy, and that still in antagonism with socialism and according to the clear indications of the historical period. But still, the great return will not occur in the consciousness of the old major national party or government, but rather in a new consciousness distinct from the old, gathered in silence and solitude.

In other words, it will occur in the nationalist consciousness of young generations. Behold the doctrine, behold finally, o gentlemen, the doctrine that the same liberalism has made necessary, while falling short of the tasks that should have been its own! Behold nationalism, behold the nationalists born, as we said, in solitude, gathered into groups of ten, grown into groups of one hundred, amidst the laughter, the negations, the accusations, the ignorance, but always advancing! All of a sudden, barely born, almost by the very act of being born, they recognize the historical positions that should have been occupied by the liberals, and they occupy them themselves. And suddenly, in full consciousness and with deliberate intent, they come together in resolute antagonism against socialism, head on, in order to wound it, not from the side, but head on. And they attack it in its two associated positions, that of the class struggle and that of the international class struggle, reawakening a love for the fatherland that by them is transmitted to others, developing a doctrine of the nation – simple and immutable laws that lead the people to create their own history and the history of the world. And onward, onward, onward! The nationalists recognize

two great events in the modern world, which are connected, mutually dependent, and both originating
from the same cause which is the greatest power of
labor and production attained by man: first of all, socialism, the imperialism of labor; secondly, colonialism, the imperialism of production and labor together,
the imperialism of peoples, the economic, territorial,
and moral expansion of the nation. And they, the nationalists, seeing again what their task is, they cross
the seas, they recognize emigration, they recognize
the necessity of it in the present conditions of Italy,
but in it and for their children they see a better,
brighter future. And over there, from those fields of
Italianity cut off from Italy, they alone, the nationalists, aware of and having understood the full extent of
their responsibilities, after Adwa, they point to
Tripoli. Historic fatality in a wholly different sense
than how the Hon. Giolitti described it, as a historical
fatality to be attained even if, in and of itself, it were
to provide no remuneration at all and was made entirely of sand and reefs, but which had to be gone
through, because the Italian people needed to pass
through it in order to begin to lift themselves up from
their state of an inferior people dispersed throughout
the world, worked by it, to the level of a greater people who improve the world by dominating it.

But onward, onward still! Nationalism reen-
ters domestic politics, wages battle for the purification of public life; this latter calls itself democracy,
while nationalism is declared the enemy of the people
and proletariat, the enemy of modern civilization and
progress. Its good friends abandon it, the good people
who once loved it do not love it anymore, its own

people forsake it, those of the democratic and anti-clerical aristocracy who before long will seek the electoral support of the sacristans; those partisans of brotherly opportunism concealed under the mystical ephod of the secret pact. And it fights against these and others. It fights against the democracy of the bloc of democratic greed, against the democracy of the joint-stock company of democratic newspapers, against the democracy of the feudal latifundismo of the democratic Roman princes. And it triumphs in the elections. But is that all there is? Only this? Did it fight, as it itself believes, only for the purification of public life? Did it fight against Freemasonry only? Did it really fight against democracy?

No, it is not like that. Nationalism has, instead, initiated a new, perfect democracy. Primarily by beginning to establish a truly democratic sovereignty, that of the Italian people in its full national totality. The nation in its organic unity, the nation, a living individuality, is sovereign. On closer inspection, all the old political parties made something else sovereign, the democrats democracy, the liberals liberty, the radicals radical politics, the socialists the proletariat, the republicans the republic, and the monarchists the monarchy. All of them, more or less, had created for themselves an abstract conception of their political credo, and that was their idol, their fetish, and their fetish naturally was their sovereign. For which reason all the parties, except socialism, paid lip service to serving the fatherland, to wanting the good of the fatherland, to putting the fatherland before everything else, but in reality there was that other sovereign, the fetish, democracy, liberty, the republic, the monarchy, civilization and the like, and the poor fatherland no longer existed. In truth then, aside from all political hypocrisy, there was only one real sovereign for our dear liberalism, democracy, and the like, and it was the individual master who sought to make a career out of political ideas. To better and more quickly understand each other, let's imagine an association in which there is an honorary president, an acting president, and then finally a man who does everything and is everything. So it was in the old democratic and liberal regime: the fatherland was, at most, the honorary president, the fetish of doctrine was the acting president, and the man who made everything happen was the selfish calculation of the democratic and liberal individual master.

Improbably, liberalism had also been diffused into our midst through the French Revolution and the rights of man, when, that is, it had already carried its doctrine to ultimate conclusions, in which the eternal struggle for predominance between the individual and society was resolved in favor of the individual and "freedom." Liberalism had become the party of the state and government, but under its public regimen its individualistic origin remained as the first presupposition of civil ethics. In that same aforementioned discourse, the Hon. Salandra reaffirmed the individualistic nature of Italian liberalism as an "expression of lineage," which, according to him, appears in the Renaissance, in the Risorgimento, and in emigration. Nor did liberalism realize the novelty that was achieved by socialism. It did not realize that socialism was returning to a solidarity, to a solidarity of class, and not only nationally, but internationally. It, liberalism, in the face of national and international organizations of socialism, remained distressingly individualistic. Nor did it ever rise again, as a serious, clear, conscious, programmatic, methodical action of party and government to the broadest and highest concept of solidarity: national solidarity. The same bourgeois organizations, in defense against socialism, were fundamentally industrial, agrarian, economic; nor did political liberalism make any effort to come into contact with them. Only one economic party remained between Milan and Turin. And in his last discourse, the Hon. Salandra will celebrate the superiority of liberal individualism over the "socialist bond," unaware of the liberal, bourgeois, national weaknesses in contrast to socialism's strength.

There was a need to return to broader and higher solidarity, to national solidarity. And from this, to the proper subordination of the individual to the nation. This was the beginning of the new, perfect democracy that we spoke of. The sovereign nation, its citizens subordinate to it. Nationalism is precisely suited to said work.

And in this and for this it arrived at the most noble of its revelations and succeeded in surrounding its political doctrine with a vital ethical and philosophical atmosphere. So that meditating on the nature of nations and seeing that these do not consist so much in some material thing, in the materiality, that is, of the prior generation, as they do in something spiritual, in the continuity, that is, of the ethical spirit through all prior generations; Italian nationalism reemerged with both an altruistic faith, as our duty towards the past and future, and a spiritualistic conception of human existence; whilst, on the other hand, liberalism continued to degenerate further into widespread materialistic degeneration, and its individualism became extremely materialistic and, applied to the management and government of the public weal, without any faith or ideal anymore; and socially and nationally materialistic it fell under the dominion of its adversary, socialism, which was and is the supreme and, we hope, final triumph of every ounce of materialism accumulated in the heart of modern men.

After which – and I'm hurrying here, ladies and gentlemen, to finish my discourse – I pose this question: Does liberalism any longer have any reason to exist? With things being, clearly, just as we have described them, does Italian liberalism have any more services left to offer Italy and can it simply die?

Well, o ladies and gentlemen, to this question we cannot respond, unless it is by posing another question, which is this: Is Italian liberalism capable of finding new material? Above all, is it capable of reforming itself morally?

A little over a year ago now, in the illustrious city where I live, I attended a rally of a great liberal political association that I belonged to. That evening the program of the then-future elections was read and needed to be discussed, and the program covered everything: freedom naturally, clericalism and secular education, the meridional question, and tax reform – all the usual stuff in short, except foreign policy. For this reason I thought it was my duty to offer a few

words and to say how, in the year of Tripoli and the
provident Mediterranean displacements, there was an
opportunity to be had, for the candidates' information
or for the electorate's instruction, a few words about
foreign and colonial policy. And so I did. But I should
never have done it! I was loudly applauded, I was *ad
litteram* covered with applause; the president, a university professor and senator of the kingdom, shouted
that he was making my proposal his own, and the assembly voted for it by acclamation. What had happened? Merely this: the good liberal people of my
city, illustrious in culture, had had need of five minutes of my time to realize, with their political consciousness, the effect of what they had been enthusi-
astic about, for many months prior, with good patriotic heart. Tripoli, beautiful land of love and all that en-
tails, did not appear to have produced political effects
worth mentioning. And on another occasion, o my
gentlemen, being in another city and giving a discourse similar to that evening, I happened to insult
my president, without realizing it, the president of the
political association that I was speaking before. Having been invited by a friend of mine, a nationalist
congressmen, and being little given to concern myself
with things that seemed insignificant to me, I had believed that the invitation made to me was for an open
gathering, or for a nationalist one; I went and I spoke.
And at a certain point, touching on the Italo-French
committee that had just been formed, I launched into
some sesquipedalian insolences against those politicians of ours who had participated. Whereupon I
heard some friends around me laugh, and someone
say "bravo" to me. But after the discourse I realized
my blunder. I had stumbled into a liberal associa-

tion's gathering, and the president, who fortunately was elsewhere at the time, had submitted his name to the Italo-French committee; his associates knew about it and were upset by my comments, but what could they do to us? And besides, that good man himself, the president, and also a congressman, had given his name just like that. To be honest, every time I hear it said that between a liberal and a nationalist there is not much difference, I think back, dear gentlemen, to the anecdote I have just recounted.

That notwithstanding, I ask myself: Can Italian liberalism fulfill its moral reformation? Can it conceive in itself the new spirit capable of nourishing it from within, the new spirit of truth and national life?

There is only one program: that of the greatness of the fatherland. That is it. But it is a program, a political program, domestic and foreign, a program of an entire political action that has for its goal the greatness of the fatherland, a program and not a patriotic aspiration, not a patriotic idealism, but a realistic program that operates from a realistic condition of the nation, its present historical state, and that aims for a realistic condition of its future historical state!

Can the Liberal Party regain its faith in this program? Can it regain its religion? Can it regain the morality that silences parliamentary egoism, dispels the fear of socialists, instills the courage of assuming responsibility, eliminates the majority of men who prove to be worthless today, and make room for the majority of worthy men who are sidelined today?

If liberalism can do this, so much the better. The nationalists, who want only one thing: to give their entire soul to their love – they will be happy to join forces with it, and liberalism will either go by the same name it goes by today, or it will change its name.

But if it cannot, they will march forward separately. For the nationalists the goal is clear, and the way is straight.

VI. Liberal State and National State[16]

The work of Italian nationalism, being muddled by daily events, does not appear today in its full clarity.

But each one of us feels, the younger more than the more experienced, each one of us feels himself to be a worker for the nation's future. In each one of us there is, in the younger more than in the more experienced, in each one of us there is a consciousness similar to that of an artist in the act of creation. We are all aware of a creation of ours involved in the general events. And for that reason we are certain that our work one day will appear in its perfect precision and magnificent importance. Without pride, but rather with a simplicity of faith, we assert that a good deal of what future generations of Italians will do is contained in us like an action, and in our nerves, before it is expressed.

What meanwhile appears evident, even in an uncertain light, is this: Italian nationalism follows a very straight line of conduct in its development, like all things that are not for men to decide, but of historical necessity. What astonishes me even more in Italian nationalism, and fills me with joy, is this: its rigorous and methodical way of proceeding. It is itself a method of revision of contemporary political values in Italy, and gradually as it applies itself it acquires an

---

[16]Original footnote: Discourse given in Rome, at the branch office of the Nationalist group, February 14, 1914.

ever greater delicacy conjoined with an ever greater penetration. We are the solvents, always going deeper, and always more corrosive of the old political formations, as we clear the way for the new political formations that we are the architects of.

Indeed, what was our first act? Horrified by the negation of our highest national purpose, foreign politics, nationalism promptly and grandly began with its propaganda for Tripoli as an affirmation of our highest national purpose. But after having dedicated itself to a first revision of domestic life accompanied by war, it immediately took on its biggest and coarsest enemy, the democratic lie, so that now look at us: at this most subtle review of our similars and allies, the liberals.

In which I believe that it is mutually beneficial for us and them to continue.

Well, how much truth is there in the aforementioned affinity between liberals and nationalists?

If you lend an ear to our friends and allies, we are nearly the same. While one leader of liberalism publicly denied our reason for existing because they themselves exist, another leader said to me in private: "I consider you as my extreme right." And everywhere, from Venice to Milan, from Milan to Turin, from Turin to Genoa, from Genoa to Naples, I heard it repeated that we are their vanguard, a well-received vanguard, especially since we have demonstrated our worth in electoral campaigns.

On the contrary, nationalists are much more reserved and moderate. We all feel that it isn't quite

the same thing. And if I should say to the very youthful nationalist generation, to that generation that is nationalist by birthright and which readily cooperates
with the socialists: "You are just a more lively cross
section of liberals," it would look at me askance and
be astonished.

How much truth is there then in the well-
known affinity between our friends and ourselves?

Well, we believe that the following can be established: that liberals and nationalists are close, but
only as people of one historical epoch that is ending
can be close to those of another historical epoch that
is beginning. Liberals and nationalists are in contact
in time and space, between them many spiritual and
political exchanges have taken place and take place,
which may give the appearance of a certain more or
less homogeneity between them, but in reality there is
between the ones and the others, as between people of
one historical epoch that is finishing and those of another that is starting, something antithetical as well.

What is the antithetical part between nationalism and liberalism? What is the antithetical part between the soul of the epoch that is finishing, from
which liberalism emerged, and the soul of the epoch
that is beginning, from which nationalism emerged?

We are, o gentlemen, a strange people with a
very strange fortune. We Italian people, for centuries
and centuries divided and subjected, we had the sad
fortune of being liberated and united with the nation
on the principles of individual rights. Italy is a people
liberated on the proclamation of the rights of man

made in France. In France, with the proclamation of
the rights of man, a class, the bourgeoisie, freed itself
from the subjugation of the other two classes, the nobility and the clergy. It is an act of social character,
the liberation of a class and, above all, the liberation
of man. It is the liberation of man on the proclamation
of the rights of man. From a social act it grows into a
national act and it is the liberation of the French people from tyranny; but still, Louis XVI loses his head
on the proclamation of the rights of man. From
France, with the Revolutionary and Napoleonic epic,
it passes to Europe, and it is the liberation of the people, but it is still the proclamation of the rights of
man. So that, when the times are ripe, even in Italy, in
this our Italy so close to France, so pervaded by
French ideas and Napoleonic rule, in this our Italy
which can never stop being French unless we agree to
throw it off; when the times are ripe, two events, the
social liberation of man and the national liberation of
the Italian people from the foreigner, are combined
or, rather, they become intertwined. Just like the earth
in the atmosphere, the so-called Italian revolution is
bathed in the entire spirit of the French revolution. I
don't need to remind you how our greater and lesser
men, men of thought and action, of conspiracy and
war, statesmen and kings, were the fathers of our revolution, especially inasmuch as they were children of
the foreign revolution.

What followed was a weakness in the formation of the Italian people into a nation, not so much
because that formation occurred under the influence
of foreign ideas, but because those ideas formed the
moral code for a social revolution and not for a na-

tional emancipation.

Well, a similar condition of things is reflected in the doctrine of liberalism, of ancient and modern liberalism, of better days and worse days, of greater and greatest men, and lesser and least men.

For all it did for the Italian constitution, for all it did for Italian history, for all the Italian goodwill it showed or shows, for all the adherents of Italian goodwill it had or has, liberalism, tragically, cannot shed, it cannot today just as it could not yesterday, it cannot shed the nature of its origins which makes of it a doctrine on behalf of the rights of man rather than on behalf of the rights of the nation. That resulted from the proclamation of the rights of man in the French fashion, when it fought for the liberation of Italy from Austria.

The conflict between the individual and society for predominance is a fundamental theme of history, much like the conflict between classes. If we, so as not lose ourselves in erudition which would be out of place here, if we limit the beginning, with respect to Italy and Europe, to the birth of Christianity, we see it, variously in Europe and variously in Italy, in various epochs, resolve itself in favor of the individual at one time, in favor of society at another. But also, from the origins of Christianity on down, through the Middle Ages, through the communes and the Renaissance in Italy, through the Reformation in other countries, through the French Revolution in all of Europe, and the world, to the present day when I am speaking to you, there is a continuous line, straight and ascending, that signals the prevalence of individualism over his adversary – society, civil society, national society, to which the individual belongs.

Well, when individualism prevails, liberalism makes laws, and for as much as it might conceive of a national soul, will, or content, for as much as it might realize a governing party, liberalism remains what it was, nor can it do otherwise, it remains the national doctrine of individualism predominating over the nation.

Do you know, friends, what Italy's specific trouble was? To have individualistic liberalism written into the foundation of its constitution. Italy was still extremely weak, it was at the weakest point in its existence, in that period of its redemption and its very early formation, and already it was coming under attack by ideas that were eroding away at it. But, as we said, our country rose up mostly in the name of eroding ideas. This is its sad fortune and this its trouble.

Neither Cavour's genius, nor that greatest father of ours having given his entire life to the holy cause, nor so many other venerable men having done the same, nor the religion of the fatherland that Mazzini shined his sublime thought on, nor the ardor of several generations, nor the blood that was shed, could conquer the spirit of the times that was within them and outside them. When it was necessary to construct Italy, they gave their genius, soul, property, life, to construct Italy without thinking of anything else, but they could not conquer the spirit of the times. They could fight and die, but, tragically, they could not conquer the spirit of the times. Which was that of the French Revolution. The entire nineteenth century seems inundated with the spirit of the French Revolution in which many things foundered, from which many things emerged. It was called the century of nationalities, and in fact more than one people was constituted, or reconstituted, into a nation, but, speaking only of ourselves, the reconstitution of the people was made on the principle of the freedom of the citizen. This freedom was the greatest thing, but it was not a national principle. Adopted as a national principle, it weakened the nation in the very act of constituting it. Adopted as a national principle, it created an antithesis that was not natural, that need not have been, between the rights of man and the rights of the state.

The Italian state resembles those creatures that have suffered in the maternal uterus so that it continues to carry around the stigmata of that suffering which it was subjected to, in the century in which it was conceived, when the individual after an effort spanning two millennia had finally triumphed over the society to which it belonged. Even at the present hour, after so many years, and after so many events and so much governance of the commonweal, the freedom of the individual, according to our liberals, if one really listens to them, appears to be the supreme end of the state, for an excessive reaction against the rule of one man, the king, who was at one time the entire state.

Today, against the new revolution of socialism, the liberal state finds in its doctrine more reason to cede than strength to resist. Its doctrine, individualistic and not national – we must be clear about this –

is good for resolving problems on behalf of the individual, not on behalf of the state or nation. This is how the problem of the relationship between society and the individual is framed, and the individual solution? – the freedom of the citizen; but what is given in compensation to the nation and to the state? Nothing. This is how the religious problem is framed, and the individual solution? – the freedom of religious practice; but what is given in compensation to the nation and to the state? Nothing. This is how the problem of class struggle is framed, and the individual solution? – the freedom to strike and to work; but what is given in compensation to the state and nation? Nothing. This is how the problem of labor organizations is framed, and the individual solution? – the freedom of labor organizations; but what is given in compensation to the state and nation? Nothing. Not even legal recognition of labor organizations which would add power to the state over them. This is how the problem of civil rights is framed, and the individual solution? – universal suffrage; but what is given in compensation to the state and nation? Nothing. One sacrifices to the lofty, abstract justices who are a sort of deity of the people against our God. Do we not need to think about the soundness of the State? But of course! Do we not need to think about the good of the nation? But of course, but of course! But it is typical of old liberalism not to notice, not to notice at all, o gentlemen, the harm it does to the nation and state, and to favor the individual, in order to increase freedom, if possible, and the rights of the citizen. Precisely because, as we said, the old form of liberalism is an individual doctrine and not a national one. For this reason it was able to give the vote to so many millions of dangerous ignoramuses, without anyone asking the question: But in the final analysis, is such a law beneficial to the state or not? No one asked! It was the citizen's due and that's that! It was sacrificed to individual justice and that's that.

Today in Italy the popular "masses" are either Catholic or socialist. The Italian state has a conflict with Catholicism, and a conflict with socialism. Nevertheless, it gives the vote to the Catholic masses and the socialist masses, without thinking of alternatives. Without thinking of arming itself with some defense against the weapon that it puts into the hand of whoever can turn around and point it at him. And if the Catholics don't do it, that only proves that Italian Catholics, in spite of the clerics and anti-clerics, are good Italian citizens; but the socialists do it. And in this way our pious priests of liberal idealism celebrate the sacred rites of lofty abstract justice, saying: "Have not all Italians without distinction fought in Libya? And all Italians without distinction have the right to vote!" But for goodness' sake, we respond, did our soldiers die in Libya for a joke perhaps, or was it for something serious? They died for something serious, the good of the fatherland, nor is it any less licit to ask for the life of a young man of twenty. And then, my gentlemen, priests of lofty justice, if the good of the fatherland has such a price that a man must die for it, when a decision needs to be made that might affect the good of the fatherland, we must keep an eye on what is good for the fatherland and on nothing else. When discussing the expansion of the vote, in other words, we should have considered whether it was beneficial to Italy at that moment and not just whether it was something owed to the citizens, and especially in memory of those who, to the contrary, were invoked to protect the rights of citizens, in memory of those who died in Libya. But of course, of course they did not fall and die down there so that a short while later in Milan, a bloody madman might be carried in triumph by twelve thousand wretches, a renegade of the fatherland among even worse foreigners. But there was a need to sacrifice to lofty justice, and the most sacerdotal among them sacrificed!

Thus conceived, or thus misconceived rather, and entirely devoid of concept and substance and right, the state can only do what we see it doing today in Italy: collapse. Until recently only, we had, if we do not still have, o friends, the strong dictatorship of the Hon. Giolitti. Eh well, for the love of our fatherland we would not want future historians to write what we think about him: which is that that dictatorship is as good as a statesman could do in the decadence of a state. We see that dictatorship as the result, on the one hand, of a concentration, in one man of extraordinary ability, of the languishing institutions of the state, from monarchy to parliament, including the bourgeois and liberal ruling classes, and, on the other hand, of a negotiation of progressive surrender with its adversaries, which appears inevitable. We see that dictatorship putting pressure on capital and industry, because labor organizations, trade unions, cooperatives, and strike organizers put pressure on it. Yesterday putting pressure on the industrialists of Turin, today on maritime companies because the sagacious power of a tribune of the sea, through the glory of the Dardanelles, presses on it. In order to disarm, in short, the greater classes, because it itself is disarmed by demagogy and by organizations of the proletariat. Not, in short, because it sits between them both as the arbitrator of happy national impartiality, but just the opposite: because it sits as best it can, partial and un-just, taking from those it fears the least in order to give to those it fears the most.

Proceeding in this way, the liberal state is at democracy now, and socialism later.

This is because socialism is the direct conse-quence of democracy, and democracy is the direct consequence of liberalism.

We are familiar with the sweet, radical democracy that we only recently saw in action in three cross sections: those who blamed the govern-ment for the deputation they had and no longer have; those who blamed the government for the deputation they do not yet have; and those who were grateful to the government for the deputation they have or hope to have. All three sections form the political party of the realization, they say, of personal deputation, with-out a hint of malignity, we add, because, on account of the greed that makes the most underhanded people ingenuous, those gentlemen practice in the open. Well: when the individual is made the center of a po-litical system, as he was in the liberal political sys-tem, ambitious degeneration is natural. "Everything must serve to make me free!" says the liberal. And the congressman of Costanzi Hall: "Everything must serve to make me a deputy!" Between these two, there may be differences of mindset and contentabili-ty, but both start from the same premise that the state exists to render them a service. And here is the rub. The dissolution of the state can result from it. Liberalism and democracy are effectively nothing but two periods of the same process of dissolution.

Again: we saw this sweet democracy that we speak of in action, with a position inside parliament and for the government, with a position outside parliament and against the government, and with a reserved position, in Palazzo Guistiniani, with a front and center seat at the labor bureau. Well, gentlemen, this last association between parliamentary bourgeois democracy and socialism may inaugurate a historical period: the historical period of the fall of the liberal state into the socialist revolution. We do not find anything that might arrest the precipitous fall of liberalism into democracy, or the precipitous fall of democracy into socialism. When the individual is made the center of a political system, just as he is made the center of the liberal political system, the two precipitous falls are contiguous. Liberal individualism devolves into individualism in its assault on power, and the two of them devolve into individualism in their assault on the present socio-economic regime. There is one premise: the state must serve! To me the liberal, it must serve to give me my freedom; to me the democrat, it must serve to allow me to lay my hands on public power; to me the socialist, it must serve to allow me to lay my hands on private wealth! But the state must serve! This is the premise of liberalism, democracy, and socialism; they spring from it like a rivulet from the same source. The rivulet is first at this point, then at that point, then at some other point along its way; and similarly liberalism, democracy, socialism are three successive stages that, departing from the same premise, lead to the same consequence which is the dissolution of the state. To argue about it is superfluous; we are in the realm of common awareness. Indeed, of common experience: it has already made the news. Men of the three stages, liberal, democratic, socialist, are mixed together before our very eyes, they are seen to cooperate in the same effort, which is to dissolve the state.

And here is the historical epoch that one hopes is coming to an end, that in which the nation was constituted on an individual principle. Here is the historical epoch that one hopes is beginning, that in which the nation has to be reconstituted on a national principle.

It is the duty of nationalism.

Nationalism is the reformer of the state.

Either nationalism has a statal soul, or it has no soul at all.

In the first place, it must be established that there is no antithesis between the state and the freedom of the citizen. It must be firmly established that the state, in order to be truly such, has no need to take away the citizen's freedom. No. In this the antithesis does not consist, between the epoch rocked by the French Revolution, and the epoch that for Italy is moved by Italian nationalism, which will earn us, God willing, a splendid revolution of our own. No, this Italian revolution of the twentieth century that succeeds the foreign revolution of the nineteenth, this Italian revolution to create the Italian state, which succeeds the foreign revolution that wanted to make citizens of the world; well, this Italian revolution that goes by the name of Italian nationalism – let it be loudly hailed for the truth and for our own justification, that it has no intention of taking away anyone's freedom. Is the free citizen today considered something of a masterwork, slowly formed over the centuries, and for that reason inviolable and sacred? Well, so be it.

Only, faced with the modern, free citizen, we need to create the modern free state.

A free citizen subordinate to a free state is our formula.

And whoever believes that there is a contradiction between the subordination of the citizen to the state and his freedom is in error.

Many believe that to recur to ancient things in order to judge the present is a leap from reality into rhetoric, but on the contrary it is they who are stuck in rhetoric. Nothing so much as the example of ancient Rome serves to help one understand how the freedom of the citizen and the freedom of the state can coexist in a just subordination of the former to the latter.

Our classical ideas, those that thrive in the popular community of culture, are in large part to be reassessed and corrected. One has to do with the relationship between the citizenry and the state: people imagine the ancient state, the classical state, in the act of assimilating once and for all that constitutive unity that is the citizen. But in reality a single, ancient state has never existed, but rather many and diverse ancients states have, and Rome was never like Sparta: it never assimilated the Romans. The Roman citizen had absolute freedom of property, the *dominus ex jure quiritium*[17] had the freedom of *uti et abuti* of his property, while the modern citizen does not. Modern private property is in a constant state of development toward one aspect of its use, that is, the public domain. The Roman citizen had absolute control over his family, the *paterfamilias* had *jus vitae et necis* over his own offspring; which is a far cry from the modern code. Moreover, let us recall the expression *civis romanus sum*[18] which affirms the sovereignty of the citizen, just as the other expression *senatus populusque romanus* affirms the sovereignty of the people. Each had a different meaning, one internal and one external: just as *senatus populusque romanus* was a sanction of domestic law, it was at the same time a invocation of the power of the Roman state to foreign peoples; just as when the Roman citizen said *civis romanus sum*, he was not only expressing his personal dignity in the world, but also another dignity, without which that first dignity could not have had any basis: the dignity of the Roman citizen before the Roman state. And this, o gentlemen, certainly could not have existed in him without his feeling a splendid freedom.

Now then, the Roman citizen having so much more freedom than we have today, where did the solidity and strength of the Roman state come from? Why did it last for so long a time, notwithstanding the

---

[17]*dominus ex jure quititium*: Latin for "master by the law of the Quirites." In other words, someone who had full and total ownership and control over a piece of property.

[18]*civis romanus sum:* Latin for "I am a Roman citizen."

plebeian encroachments and the democratic transformation? Already the class struggle is burning brightly at the origins of the republic, and from these origins on down it is a complete advancement of the plebs over the patricians, of democratic princes over aristocratic ones. The institution of the tribunate dates from 494 B.C. In 445 the prohibition of matrimony between patricians and plebs is abrogated. In the same year, the plebs assault the institution of the consulate which is in the hands of the patricians; already in 367 one of the consuls is from the plebs, and in 172 both. Already in 366 there is no longer any distinction between patricians and plebs insofar as the right of holding a seat in the senate. And in 356 the first plebeian dictator appears. And already in 350 the plebs, on a par with the patricians, are *possessores agri publici*.[19]

So what strength, what good substance, endured in the Roman state?

Aristocratic thought, from rustic and patrician origins.

Which consisted simply in this: that the Roman state was born healthy, was born with a very robust physical, statal constitution, was born like a being with its own life, functions, and aims. And therefore it could give and gave to its citizens, to every citizen in its individual entity, the maximum of freedom, like the human body and any living body, giving the maximum freedom to its constituent units which are perfect organisms in themselves. So citizens were constitutive, free units and at the same time subordi-

---

[19]*Possessores agri publici*: Latin for "possessors of public lands."

nate to the vast functioning body. Such "theory" is strong in the instinct of the Roman state. And for that reason alone it could endure for a long time and advance in its conquest of the world, before the democratic degeneration undid it and left it to be reformed under tyranny.

And this, friends, is the ancient, eloquent example for our modern necessity.

This is the task of nationalism in the new epoch: to develop within the state the state's own thought, in other words, that the state is living for the state, that the nation is living for the nation, and that Italy is, in short, living for Italy; and finally that the state is the visible form of its life. Not the visible form of life for the individual, but for Italy; not for the individual's freedom, as the liberals say, but for Italy; not for democracy, or in order to realize democracy, as the radicals say, but for Italy; not for the class, or for the redemption of the proletariat, as the socialists say, but for Italy. Redemption of the proletariat, yes; democracy, yes; freedom, yes; but, for the state, this is the minimum program that it must work into, and not against, its maximum program, which is Italy.

"Italy? Italy, you say? And don't we say the same thing ourselves? We are all nationalists!" It seems to me that I can hear the voice of our dear friend and ally, the liberal. "We are all nationalists!" It is the courteous exclamation of those who wish us well and simultaneously declare that we are perfectly useless, merely because they exist. But I reply to our dear friend and ally: "My liberal friend, I have given a long speech to demonstrate that men say something else, that their good will is something else, their work something else, the political principles that their spirits are ruled by are something else. I have given a long speech, and I don't wish to repeat myself. You who say you are a nationalist, take a first look at yourself and see whether your will corresponds with your words, and if so, take a second look at yourself and see whether your works correspond with your will, and if so, take a third look at yourself and see whether your political principles correspond with your works. And if the answer is yes, conclude that you no longer have, and have never had, liberal principles, and that you have ours instead – jump over the divide and come with us. Here you will find yourself among your redeemed contemporaries and among the youth who are nationalists since the time they were weaned off their mother's breast for the provident reactions that a providential law rouses throughout generations, so that the order of things which have been disturbed might be re-established and must continue. Then, all our truth and yours will be made manifest to you: as much to say that you will have already passed over from the old epoch of liberalism to the new epoch of nationalism. Jump over the divide! Because finally we wish to conclude that even liberalism can continue to live, but only provided that it is reborn in nationalism, just as the Christians said of the pagans, when they converted; they said that they were reborn in Christ. Jump over the divide then, liberal friend!"

This is one of the fundamental truths on which we begin our magnificent construction. The truth of the national state.

And once again, a political doctrine returns to proclaim to the world that the state is either aristocratic, or it is not.

Ours is a mixed system, democratic and aristocratic both; it is democratic in its acceptation of the continual renewal of values, nationally and imperialistically, [being] profoundly democratic in this, according to world laws; but it is aristocratic in its conception of the state that within itself it works for its own ends.

Once again we return to proclaim to the world that the liberal state, the democratic state, the socialist state are all degenerations of that same state. It may grant freedom, accept democracy, even implement socialism potentially; but insofar as it is a state, if it does not want to betray itself, it cannot be a state that tolerates any adjectives, except one: national.

And in this the state is aristocratic. Because the same nation is aristocratic in nature inasmuch as it is spiritual in nature.

And behold another fundamental truth of Italian nationalism, the spirituality of the nation, just as the other truth is the necessity of the international class struggle.

With these three truths, national state, struggle, and spirituality, nationalism revives politics entirely, in both thought and action.

And with these same truths it can put Italy on the path toward a greater history. With its statal truth it can give it the body, with its international truth, it can give it the action, with its spiritual truth it can give it the ultimate purpose. The purpose of transforming that portion of the world where its virtue and fortune will want its civilization to spread, instilling values of the spirit instead of the materialistic values that reign today.

Much of this is left up to you, o youth, because you are the generation between us and the future. Having been born in a period when even royal children came onto the scene when mortifying ideas were being bandied about, the most capable among us did our utmost to disseminate their grand and austere ideas amidst blindness, enticements, and derision. And they have had their reward for being able to consign it to you, the reagent generation, like the soldier who passes the watchword to the next soldier on the battlefield.

It is now up to you to do the rest. Do as with the brief word that gives rise to immense music. And in that way you must fill all this age with the profound ardor of your faith, and from it the future will be born according to our hope.

Until now, we have always sought to be near to the people, because the people have a feeling for those national and aristocratic things that we have spoken about; but until now it has not really been possible, because there are common adversaries between them and us. We will continue to seek the good expedient, but we do not know if we will succeed.

For you, it is more likely that, if the error does not pass today, it will pass tomorrow. You could then draw near to the people, to redeem them and to have them with you.

And then all of Italy will fight for Italy.

VII. Nationalism and Socialism[20]

Two very great events of the modern world, commonly considered contrary to one another, are, instead, very similar and arise from the same cause. They are indeed at odds, but they are also very similar and arise from the same cause. These two great events are modern socialism and modern imperialism. They are so similar, they partake in fact so much of the same nature, that the name of the one is sufficient to denominate the other because socialism is itself a form of imperialism: it is an imperialism of class, while the other, properly called, is today what it has always been: the imperialism of nations.

The same cause from which they both arose, as we have said, o listeners, was the greatest force of work and production achieved by man, between the end of the eighteenth century and the course of the nineteenth. The primary cause was the mechanization of production and the mechanization of transportation on land and sea. The first increased production, the second increased global trade by shortening distances. The English weaver from 1819 to 1846 nearly quintupled his annual average production of cloth; and the iron produced by England rose from 442,000 tons in 1823 to 2,093,000 tons in 1848; the quantity of coal transported from one port in England to the other or abroad rose from 4,803,000 tons in 1820 to

[20]Original footnote: Discourse given at the Università Popolare di Milano, January 14, 1914, then in Bologna, Padua, etc.

11,381,000 tons in 1849, and the importation of foreign wool for English factories, in the same time period, more than quadrupled. Then, regarding commercial development due to the railroads and steam navigation, consider these figures alone: while English exports for Eastern India since 1860 or thereabouts was from 6 to 7 million pounds sterling, after several years, thanks to the railroads constructed there by the English, it reached 17 million.

Thus began, for the productive couple, that is, for the productive worker and the productive capitalist, the greatest period in history, and their importance in the world was unparalleled. When one of the two, the worker, revolted against the other, the capitalist, socialism arose, which not only gave to the worker the awareness of his greater value, not only promised to elevate him to a greater moral and economic condition, but even offered him the seignory over civil society, teaching him how to transform it into his image and resemblance, after having completely destroyed capitalism.

Which in its industrial and commercial form meanwhile put pressure on the European states and prompted them to intensify or begin their commercial expansion. The greater nations, like England and France, but also the lesser ones, like Belgium, and even those like Spain, fallen from their level of greatness and recently stripped of the last remnants of their centuries-old empires, threw themselves on Africa and Asia; and where they had colonies, they expanded them, and where they didn't, they conquered them. Some acted by imitation, all acted according to the law which they were inexorably subjected to, striving to be equals in power as much as possible, but the new impulse that, overtly or covertly, directly or indirectly, spurred the first group the most, which pulled the others in tow, arose from the great vehemence of production, voracious for space.

It is superfluous to observe that, in the reality of things, imperialism is as much a fact of proletarianism as it is of capitalism; in the reality of things, the worker, before earning a wage, is the copartner of the boss; he is the copartner standing beside the office machinery, alongside the railway, on board the steamer that traverses the Ocean, in the transcontinental market. In the reality of things, the worker and the boss are bound in the consortium of production before they are competitors in distribution. In different, but equivalent ways, each has its fortune bound up with the fortune of production, its commerce and its trade. And by consequence, as we have said, in the colonial expansion, or imperialism, of the nation to which they belong. The English worker is well aware that across the boundless English empire of five continents, when an action takes place, it involves him as well, on a daily basis, and it has a profound effect on his domestic budget: it is the immense English commerce strictly dependent on English imperialism. The worker in London is well aware that Egypt and the Cape of Africa and India and Canada and Australia have contributed and contribute to elevating his well-being and primarily to propagating it by an always greater number of English workers and English citizens.

Nonetheless, socialism suppressed productive,

industrial, commercial, colonial, imperialistic cooperation, the cooperation between the proletariat and capitalism, which has the world as its playing field, and
organized only their competition, the struggle of the
pair competing for distribution at the entrance to the
workshop. Thus, every interaction between the two
producers was reduced to that of their struggle standing beside the machinery, while from there to the extreme ends of the earth an act of extraordinary vehemence and power developed, the entirety of modern
industrial capitalism, not only that, but the entirety of
the colonialism of modern nations which depended on
cooperation, on a community of interests, on the con-
sequent solidarity and shared corresponsibility of
those two same producers who were at each other's
throat. A grandiose phenomenon of dramatic violence
and tragic terribility never again to be seen in history,
which the world was the stage to: fate appeared to ag-
itate men's productive forces in order to punish them
with their fecundity beyond all recorded limits, and at
the same time to urge them even beyond the exasper-
ation of their energy. Industrialism, having become
one with colonialism, became one with the foreign
policy of various nations; it renewed national programs, it created new national positions, it laid down
the conditions for new oppositions and new ententes
with other nations. It was the beginning, in short, of a
new, immense chapter in the national history of
greater and lesser European peoples. It transformed itself, in short, into the action of peoples and states beyond their borders, an action that, moreover, was well
deserving of human civilization, because it reclaimed
continents from savage sterility. And yet, while industrialism effected this abroad, domestically, under

the workshop roof, beside the machinery, the copart-
ner-turned-adversary, the competitor-turned-antago-
nist, held it in its grip by menacing life and property.
It created the strike in order to suppress industrialism
at the beginning of its labor, at the source of its production: it created international class organizations in
order to oppress it with all the strength in the world.
Above all, it assailed it in the policies of states that it
had animated and with which it had been conjoined: it
assailed it in colonialism, or imperialism. Large-scale,
modern industrialism was nationalized through imperialism; and its enemy, socialism, in order to oppose
imperialism, dissociated itself from the nation. Imperialism was the expansion of the nation; and socialism
became the party of systematism and, I would almost
add, of official opposition to any program of national
expansion.

Now, in Italy there was a moment when this
party had come out on top, and it had won not so
much because of its own strength but because it found
allies everywhere, in all parliamentary politics, in all
the parties and men favored by the people. It was the
moment following the Battle of Adwa. At that time,
our Italy lay at the depths of its misery; defeated, dis-
credited in Europe, humiliated, with a monarchy initially aghast, bleeding afterwards, with a state reduced to an administration, with all the decrepitude of
the ruling classes and all its traditions from servile
times which were frenetically and, I might almost say,
obscenely reacting against the attempt at greatness
made by a single man, their being drunk with oppro-
brium. Italy appeared near the end of its rope as a nation, reduced to a poor people that was proliferating

in order to emigrate. One party alone was thriving then in Italy, it was a force in the full flower of youth, and this party was socialism. But socialism acted for itself and for the proletariat, it did not act for the nation. And everything else was death, debilitation, and cowardice.

With Italy being this way, Italian nationalism was born. And it was born in reaction to all that. The first time it had consciousness of itself, it realized in itself a movement of instinctive revolt against everything that was or was happening around it. The Abyssinia War had not been driven by any sort of Italian imperialism with Italian industrialism exuberant for production standing behind it; it had not been an episode of that great phenomenon of modern colonial mercantilism that we spoke about earlier; it had been a colonial venture by imitation, because Italy had followed the example of other, greater colonizing nations; and it had been above all the brainchild of a pioneering political genius. Nor in that, or because of that, could the two gigantic champions of the epoch, as already mentioned, be found combatting each other – proletarian socialism and national mercantile imperialism, namely. It was not your typical struggle. Because, as we have already pointed out, and as, moreover, everyone of us remembers, o listeners, socialism had emerged as the victor at that time, not alone, but in company, and not only with other popular parties, or populist parties, but with all that various but not too diverse Italy of the constituted, ruling order – parliamentary, bourgeois, and monarchic – which well deserved the definitions just now applied to it. And for that reason, in the beginning, our nationalism was not a pure movement against the Socialist Party, but was against *this* and against whatever had united with it to end the war with defeat. It was a movement of revolt against the living force that still seemed to exist in Italy, and to dominate Italy, and against all the other dead forces that seemed to remain in order to make it submissive. It was against revolution and conservatism.

And in the beginning nationalism was merely a cry of grief for defeat and even more for the shame of a war that ended abruptly. It was a cry of grief by the Italian soul that had once again invoked victory, the mother of nations, and had once again seen it slip away.

Such a character of military pathos, of tragic warrior religiosity, was had by Italian nationalism at its origins.

But then it quickly developed and took a broader and more complex turn. In brief, it became one and the same with that part of Italy that was rising up, was the effect of it, and was, in turn, both the instigator and the accelerator of it. One part of Italy was rising up, or rather it was standing up for the first time economically, productively, becoming less poor by means of progressive industrial and commercial activity. It was the new Italy of labor and production, frugality and saving, physical and moral health, which was preparing for an uplifting of spirits that should have led to a upturn, with greater means, of Italian politics in Europe. Several years after Adwa, anyone endowed with a certain degree of sensibility in the matter could see the first signs that that upturn, sooner or later, was going to happen, could be in some way a precursor [of things to come]. And [latent] nationalism was this precursor. Having embraced economic Italy, which was making progress, it was the precursor, and both the cause and the effect, and the sensibility and the voice, of political and national Italy, which was slowly rising up.

In reality, nationalism had, for some time, embraced the productive part of the Italian people, the proletarian and bourgeois part, had concerned itself with social matters and with the class struggle. But to be perfectly honest, except in certain moments of indecision and confusion easily explainable in a new doctrine, it never took sides, was never for the bourgeoisie or against the proletariat. Indeed, among some of its more notable followers and that reformation of socialism called syndicalism, there was a reciprocation of tender feelings; nor did the first shy away from conceiving of a future national systematization similar to a large trade union, composed of so many smaller labor unions. And without exception, every nationalist saw in the people, in the proletariat of the factories and of the fields, the positive force, the generative and fecund force, the great breeding ground of youth where civil virility thrives, and in this lies the moral of the distinction between the classes, not closed like castes in ancient times, but open in a modern sense and more like social conditions than classes, which one might exit in order to ascend, or descend, with respect to life's vigor which increases or decreases. Never, I repeat, with such ethical principles, could nationalism be, nor was, anti-proletarian, in order to be bourgeois.

It was, instead, in favor of the superior morality of the superior organism. It was then and is now vehemently opposed to socialism of any political, messianic, or demagogic character, which, by too greatly confusing the bourgeoisie with the state or the state with the nation, did not hesitate to strike at the nation while aiming to strike at the bourgeoisie. In other words, nationalism aligned itself early on against the Socialist Party; insofar as the latter, with its specific goal of exalting a class, had become, as we called it, the party of systematic and official opposition to any possible program to enlarge the Italian nation. And in that respect, nationalism was the antagonist: it was, if we must apply a term of militant politics to it, the particular party of propaganda for the expansion of the Italian nation.

Essentially, even in Italy, sooner or later the historical period of the two great twin and conflicting phenomena had to begin, one of which obeyed the law of production and the other of distribution. Nationalism drew near the former; it was for the law of production that tends to expand, in Italy, always in the secure, steadfast, and sincere essence of its doctrine, if not yet in its pragmatic declarations; it was the first affirmation and first vanguard of modern imperialism.

And so, with us, even the law of distribution, acting by means of the class struggle that closes national life within the confines of domestic politics, like a man left to die in the arena, it had its champion in socialism; and the law of production that reaches its maximum development in national imperialism had its champion in nationalism. Tripoli is still not, for Italy, the enterprise of an imperialism that has a vigorous mercantilism as its driving force, but it is already more so than Eritrea, without comparison; and besides, the nationalists were the only ones who saw in it more of an opportunity for greater production by a larger Italian population than merely the coast whose possession reestablishes the political equilibrium of the Mediterranean. Or rather, they too ascribe the greatest importance to this equilibrium, but not in the static sense of historic destiny in the style of Giolitti and so many parliamentarian liberals, huge patriots perhaps, but in the dynamic and productive sense instead; that is, the aforementioned equilibrium offers Italy a good point of departure to advance for its own benefit. The equilibrium is a kind of solidarity. Now, we are not aware of a Mediterranean solidarity, but a Mediterranean position for our own benefit.

Therefore, after Tripoli, nationalism will continue to develop its program which is precisely this: to lift the Italian nation up out of its historical present, which is even still one of international inferiority, to a historical period of superiority. This rise is just now underway, and needs to continue.

I have often been been pleased to use socialist expressions. I stay in contact with this formidable adversary as much as possible, and I do it consciously because the two doctrines, socialism and nationalism, are both products of the same epoch, and the second arose as a direct result of the first. With such considerations in mind then, I once defined nationalism in a way that my closest and most intimate nationalist friends did not understand, and they thought that I was speaking ironically, whereas instead I was speaking with the utmost seriousness and meant to say precisely what I had said. The definition then of nationalism was this: it is the socialism of the Italian nation in the world.

I stand by that definition.

And I will explain myself, o gentlemen.

Capital is not just a national matter, it is also, and precisely, an international matter. It does not just act, it does not just dominate, from one class to the next, but it acts, it dominates, from one nation to the next as well. It is an old truth that several years ago felt, and even today feels, like a discovery. And when historical materialism, specially adopted by socialist writers, sought and found the economic substrate of all the exploits of all peoples and the competition between them and their wars, it was merely documenting an old truth that today has become a discovery.

What is the reasoning of socialism, in a nutshell? It is this: the proletarian class is deprived of a portion of the wealth that belongs to it, because that portion is unjustly held by the capitalist bourgeoisie. It is the theory of surplus value.

But with this theory there is actually another theory, a doctrine, which has for its purpose to create a morality that serves, pardon me the expression, as a platform for the demands of the proletariat, and provides them a complete arsenal of weapons for their victorious war. But the doctrine does not hold water, and the morality is purely about class.

There is something more exalted and more solid and more profound in socialism, and it is the recognition that the proletarian class is deprived of a portion of the wealth that could belong to it, but does not belong to it, because society is now organized in such a way that the capitalist bourgeoisie are able to hold on to it, whether it belongs to them or not. There is, in short, the pure and simple recognition of this fact: that the distribution of wealth is strictly dependent on social organization. And it is precisely this social organization that needs to be changed to arrive at a change in that distribution.

Eh, well, who will not acknowledge then that there is an entire international organization of nations that bring about a distribution of wealth, from one nation to the next, similar to what socialism has recognized between classes? Who will not acknowledge that the accumulation of hundreds upon hundreds of billions made by one nation within its natural borders limits the enrichment of another, adjacent nation that within its own borders has gathered only twenty or thirty? Who will not acknowledge that in the realm of international business the position of global banker, which only two nations, France and England, have attained, is a privileged position with respect to that of other nations, their customers, or patrons with respect to their clients? Who will not acknowledge that England's sending of gold to find gold in those same regions where Italy is forced to send emigrants to find work and wages, who will not acknowledge that, this being the case, there exists a civil state of some nations that socialists would call bourgeois, as opposed to a civil state of other nations that socialists would call proletarian? In short, yes, o listeners, who will not acknowledge that just as there are proletarian classes that are such because they are the dependents of other classes that are bourgeois, there are also proletarian nations that are such because they are the dependents of other nations that are bourgeois?

And so Italy is still a proletarian nation in Europe, and it had need of its socialism. And this is precisely, as we said, nationalism. In short, it is necessary to recognize this truth which is so simple: that there are two fields of distribution, one small and one large; the small one is the nation, the distribution between class and class, by means of the class struggle, organizations, strikes, and lockouts; the second is the world, the distribution between nation and nation, by means of the international class struggle, markets, colonies, ships, and cannons.

Herein lies the essence of Italian nationalism.

Which, in the end, o listeners, makes the socialists' morality its own and with all its heart, not precisely that of surplus value, but what is based on a more exact, more solid, and profounder knowledge.

Socialism is all about the effort to produce a social change. It speaks in order to arrive at an equality, or rather, at a unification of the classes, but this is its messianic vision which is outside the scope of what, with forceful metaphor, we might call the historical future. On the other hand, we appreciate socialism for its direct effort to produce a change in the possession and rule by the bourgeoisie over the proletariat. It is a change from today's inequality which is in the bourgeoisie's favor, to tomorrow's inequality which is in the proletariat's. It is, in other words, a change founded not on a particular theoretical morality, but on that universal morality that, continually in motion, moves not only human societies, but all living things in the world. It is the morality even that we ourselves asserted when we justified the distinction between the classes, inasmuch as such distinction makes the renewal of productive energies possible from bottom to top. Since such energies in the native *humus* of popular classes continually form and reform, while little by little they are exhausted in the classes that already have possession and dominion. And it is necessary that newly-formed energies rise to take the place of old ones, in order to continue the possession and dominion that now awaits them by right and duty: by right, as the reward of conquest, by duty, inasmuch as they, the possession and dominion, that is, serve and must serve to produce.

For this reason, they are always cohesive with productive energies, and when these latter tend to diminish they tend to abandon them. Such is the universal morality for individuals, families, classes, nations, and empires.

Would socialism like to be an application of it with respect to society and, more specifically, the classes? And nationalism an application of it with respect to Italian nationalism. There is, in short, a system of classes that make up Italy, and the socialists say: "A revolution is needed in order to pull up the proletarian class." Their act is a strike. But there is also a system of nations that makes up Europe, and the nationalists say: "A certain amount of revolution is needed in order to pull up Italy." And they justify war as the means. Regarding the war of Tripoli, the great poet, now dead, Giovanni Pascoli,[21] said it well, when he exclaimed: "The great proletariat has stirred!" What did he mean by that? He wanted to point out just how much similarity there was in that war of the humble, patient, and tireless mother of emigrants and workers of the world [i.e., Italy] – to the proletarian uprising. Recall then, listeners, what happened next: we had not only Turkey, but all of Europe against us. Why? What had happened? What had we done wrong? We had struck at the great banking [system], the mercantile, plutocratic bourgeoisie of Europe. The great proletariat had struck at the European nations' social system, and it reacted.

One can actually think of Europe as one great nation in which each particular nation is like a class within a nation with respect to the others. The European nations can be classified, in the precise meaning of the word; they can be, that is, valued and distinguished by their reciprocal position just as classes are valued and distinguished by their reciprocal position.

Above all, there are two nations, two only, but not just in Europe – in the world; two nations that have accumulated within their borders a wealth that is greater than their needs. They act, as we said, like the bankers of other nations, and, as we said, they are France and England. Traditionally enemies, today they are united by the calculation to maintain their

---

[21]Giovanni Pascoli: Italian writer and poet (AD 1855-1912), one of whose works, *Dark Minerva,* is published by Sunny Lou Publishing, 2022.

unique position with maximum exploitation. France is an immense bank with a capital of from 280 to 300 billion, England an immense bank with a capital of from 350 to 400 billion. While they have more capital than their needs, other nations have less.

Germany, although a very strong producer, has less. It is the typical, huge, industrial enterprise under intense development.

Italy is even less productive, with a wealth of from 80 to 85 billion, inferior to that of Austria-Hungary itself which is from 120 to 130. Italy, half of which is lying in a much humbler condition, with an emigration that this year alone will exceed one million, is even closer to the condition of the proletariat, just as Germany is already closer to becoming rich.

Then there are, finally, the extremely poor nations [of Europe], and their archetype is the Balkans.

If we wish to convince ourselves that this classification of European nations corresponds to a correct conception, one might consider that the same exact thing happens to them as happens to classes: each has an expansion, or domination in the world, commensurate with its economic position. The two greatest empires are the English and the French. The French empire, patrimony of the French nation, spans 10 million 113 thousand square kilometers across five continents, and the English empire spans 29 million. These are, as I said, the global patrimonies of the two greatest nations in terms of culture and otherwise.

If however we wish to gain a deeper understanding of the facts that we are discussing, let us ex-

amine another sort of French empire: let us examine
the moral empire that the French exercise over the
world, and let us examine it specifically in relation to
Italy. Collecting the entire complex of possible ex-
pansions and areas of domination of a people under
the denomination of "civilization's influence," we see
that the influence of French civilization is over-
whelming compared to Italian civilization. And one is
forced to admit it even without leaving Italy. But anyone who goes to South America has an even more
poignant sensation of it, if that is possible, seeing
with his own eyes all that is happening. There, they
have an extreme need for Italian labor; there, Italian
labor provides an immense product, but it is proletarian and it is a commodity, whereas what is French is
highly esteemed. The culture of Buenos Aires, if it
has one, and that of Rio de Janeiro which has one, are
both French, like ladies' fashion. Which fashion is of
course a frivolity, o listeners, but it is also one of the
many indicators of the expansion and domination of
one people over other peoples. And the French dominate us in all respects: in frivolity, in language, in
money, in thought. The wealth in Tunisia is French,
and the labor is Italian. The wealth in Argentina is
French, or English, and the labor is Italian. There, in
Argentina, Italian labor stands below, and above it is
French wealth, and further above that is French civilization. As it is in Argentina, so is it in Tunisia. The
French dominate us in every way. Except for procreation which they reduce to enjoyment, thus hastening
to break down the ethical relationship between man
and what he possesses which is his productive energy,
his capacity, and his instinctive will to produce. And
you see, o listeners, the terrible fact! Morality offend-

ed, the inexorable cosmic law, violated, is avenged. As can be seen in a small book worthy of serious study, a book by Professor Corrado Gini of the University of Padua – France, becoming depopulated, devalues its own soil, loses energy in its industries; that is, at the height of its wealth today, it already tends toward impoverishment. It tends toward diminishment. And where a nation diminishes, another nation intervenes, precisely like class to class.

Such knowledge reinforces the essential [need for] Italian nationalism.

But someone will close himself off in a sort of prejudice and say: it is not possible to classify nations, because a juridical state does not exist for nations, and they are independent of each other, while the Italian proletariat and the Italian bourgeoisie are two classes bound together by one juridical state within one nation, a national system, a system that makes the exploitation of one over the other both possible and legal. One needs, therefore, to break the system, to abolish the juridical state, which is precisely what socialism proposes to do.

Well, o listeners, if in Europe there is not a juridical state, there is something else in its stead that tends to have ever more efficacy, and it is the new and old internationalist moralism, internationalism understood as the natural solidarity of humanity, pacifism, and everything like it that is being preached today, and it is done on purpose for the conservation of the *statu quo* of the present global arrangement which is all in favor of the people who have more, all against those who have less. The juridical state is the consolidation of a moral state that was previously formed and which was already in its day an initial consolidation of property. Now, if in Europe one is still quite far from the law of *statu quo*, we would already like to sanction the morality of it, thanks to internationalist ideas, excellent for the global bankers, the English and the French, and even for the greatest producers, the Germans, but terrible for the proletariat, us. From the Balkan War we saw conservative nations of the *statu quo* most busy at limiting it. The same nations created the ephemera Albania, and when this latter began to be lacerated, the same nations for the same reason of conservation, by now organic to them, let it be lacerated. They watched and will watch, without lifting a finger, the war and the butchery of unarmed people. It is plutocratic, financial, and industrial pacifism, the vertiginous purveyor of arms, and by the same calculation whereby it purveys arms to them, it is the abolisher of wars. Which can be accepted by other nations because of their minority, because of impotence, because of ethnic weakness, not unlike that of the proletarian class before socialism came along and made it "evolved and aware," in other words, a fighting army.

Armed pacifism is the European juridical state; that is, it is the expedient of power wherewith the richest nations dominate the poorer ones. They dominate them in two ways, by imposing peace and by imposing arms. With peace, the greater nations conserve what they think best to conserve, their empires spreading from 10 to 30 million square kilometers, and their strongboxes containing from 300 to 400 billion. With armaments, they afflict the smaller

and much poorer states in their domestic life. And
when the Socialist Party attacks the state and the
bourgeoisie, rebuking them for their military spend-
ing, it practices a policy for its own purposes and use,
ignoring, or pretending to ignore, reality. It is not the
Italian state, it is not the Italian bourgeoisie that wants
to augment its armies and navies, but foreign nations:
Austria, France and the others. There is an international interdependence that regulates the proportion-
ment of national armies and navies. This interdependence obliges Italy to have such and such an army
and such and such a navy. In other words, foreign nations exert on Italy an influence of greatest domestic
character; they penetrate intimately into its domestic
life, into its domestic economy, into the arrangement
of the relationship between its financial potential and
the systematization of its budget. In other words, all
Italian interests, the interests of property, labor, production, and therefore all the political relations among
classes, of proletarianism and capitalism, and therefore the very conditions of the class struggle, the entire domestic life, economic and political, of Italy, of
the people and of the state, and of its constitutive
units, individuals and classes – they are all subject to
the actions and influences of foreign nations. The
most internal, the most intimate aspect of our national
life, the tax system, is under the control of foreign nations. According to a French parliamentary report, in
1905 the land tax in France produced 146,546,000 L.
In Italy, it rose to 250 million. While the area of
France is a little less than double that of Italy, and the
cultivatable area is more than double. Comparatively
in terms of taxes, France ought to pay 500 million,
but it pays only 146. Well, one cannot help thinking

that the great, excessive tributary pressure by the Italian state on its subjects is due to an international pressure, by the above-mentioned international interdependence. In this way, foreign nations succeed in devaluing in our own country what most belongs to us, the land itself, inasmuch as the inexorable necessity of keeping them at bay constrains us to subject it to too heavy a tax burden. And as with the land, so too with the other great branch of production, industries, whose development can be retarded or impeded. In fact, many Italian industries complain of being oppressed by excessive fiscal burdens and being unable to grow because of it. Well, one cannot help thinking that this happens because of the international interdependence of rich nations being oppressive to poor nations.

Well, Italy has a voice that informs it of all that. That voice is precisely nationalism.

It rests on solid foundations, as we have seen, and on eternal principles: the ethnic principle, inalienable and eternal like the individual principle, as well as the principle of natural development of the ethnic organism in the world, a development no less natural than that of the individual organism.

The more nationalism is based on the principle of production that exceeds distribution in terms of power and utility, the more it meets the greater needs of man and the species.

Finally, o listeners, by now we all see that the socialist distribution has become destructive. It is no longer distribution, but destruction. Destruction of the productive forces of land and industry, destruction of national power, destruction of the civilization of the world even. You know in fact, o listeners, that not too long ago, due to political malevolence, due to abominable demagogy, the Milanese socialists prohibited labor cooperatives from going to Libya. By doing so they wanted to keep the proletariat hostile to that conquest of the Italian nation, and that would be enough to condemn them; but they did more than that, they cut off for their own benefit the passage of civilization that was in progress from one continent to the other. Whereby, on account of the monstrous demagogues of Alta Italia, if all our workers were similar to those of their slave cooperatives, and if the same had happened in France and England and among other peoples, Africa would still remain not much different from America before Christopher Columbus sailed the ocean and discovered it and offered it to the working family of the human race.

In this way the socialists destroy national and international production, and they envy the world its population and civilization; they are two times – you will pardon me this expression which appears declamatory, but it is not – they are two times Malthusian with respect to the human race.

In opposition to which stands our law, the law of production, the law of the nation and universal humanity.

And if Italy is destined not to lose its way, nor the ends of the earth to grow dark, then the former will prevail over the latter.

VIII. Tripolitania, the Balkans, the Turco-European Plutocracy[22]

The Italo-Turkish peace, whether it still exists or not, and the great powers' effort to extinguish the Balkan flare up, whether this effort succeeds or not, suggests several considerations to me.

The considerations rest on two facts.

The first fact has accompanied nearly the entire period of our war [in Libya]; the second regards the Balkans and the great powers.

The first is as follows. In France, in the smaller cities in the countryside, in the atriums of the branches of French banks, the Bank of France, the Crédit Lyonnaise, telegrams from the war were displayed. They were always those from a Turkish source and printed in very large characters. Those from an Italian source were not displayed because during the day there were those from the Turkish source, while in the evening the branch offices were closed and by the time morning rolled around again other messages of new Turkish victories were prepared.

It was in this way that they succeeded in not spooking the French capital of the provinces that was invested in Turkey.

---

[22]Original footnote: October 11, 1912.

In the larger cities, like Bordeaux and Lyons, it was the same. Telegrams from a Turkish source printed in large characters. Only, in the evening, because the succursals in those cities remained open, on the walls of the atriums there appeared a tentative strip with, above it, written in small characters, this note: "*This news is unconfirmed.*" Only rarely, an even more tentative telegraph from an Italian source appeared, in even smaller characters.

As for Paris, anyone who has followed even superficially from a distance the Parisian newspapers is capable of understanding that it was the driving force behind that great machine seen in action in Autun, for example, and in Rouen, Bordeaux, and Lyon. The traditional and well-known trope of Italian imbellicosity, a trope that the French were primarily responsible for spreading throughout Europe, as a result of an uninterrupted series of documents beginning with the centuries-old depiction of a particular dispute between a frog and a Lombard, which Professor Vittorio Cian references in his recent, respectable opusculum, and ending with that contemporary one found on Franco-Chinese postcards which Guilio De Frenzi recently brought to the attention of readers of the *Giornale d'Italia*: spreading the old gratuitous assertion that "Italians do not fight" and the like; this trope, dusted off and put back into circulation for the occasion, is on the one hand, even today, an outburst of sentimental malevolence, and on the other, today, one cannot help suspecting that it was, during our war, a practical auxiliary to the bank telegrams from a Turkish source. The popular tradition of Italian imbellicosity explained the Turkish victories from a Turkish source and thus contributed to reassuring count-less French provincials, the little capitalists of great French capital invested in Turkey.

We come now to the second fact that I mentioned regarding the Balkans and the great powers. The readers are well aware of it.

Readers cannot fail to have observed that the intervention of the great powers in Constantinople and the Balkan capitals was originally planned by Paris. The initiative was taken by the French prime minister, and the first arrangement was between him and the Russian minister Sazonov, who happened to be in Paris at the time. Russia is politically allied with, but capitalistically indebted to, France, and such subjection of the great empire to a democratic republic is the supreme example wherein the grandiose deceit of contemporary so-called democracy is revealed. The prodigious plutodemocratic republic forces its democratic lesser half to bind to that absolute empire which its plutocratic greater half itself binds to. One cannot help supposing that the Russian minister in Paris, without even realizing it, was led, by the influence of local circles, to seek out the means to impede the breakout of war in the Balkans, together with Poincaré who was undoubtedly the more-or-less conscious public agent of those plutocratic circles. It is certain that France's Turkish policy today is plutocratic and not national. That frantic activity by France, more than that by others, which we have seen in recent days was not a rush to the defense of national interests, but rather to the defense of plutocratic ones. The fact is that France has recently had the well-merited honor of taking the lead in Europe by its effort to settle the Oriental question, and to impress on this settlement and on this decrepit question the strong plutocratic character of its republic. Thus, the intervention of the great powers in the Balkans, the impediment of war, the Ottoman *statu quo*, the European policy of European peace – they are all, on a grand scale, what the telegrams from a Turkish source concerning the Libyan War and the traditional discredit generously thrown with both hands on the Italian soldier were, on a small one. They are expedients designed to put capital's mind at ease.

The two facts are these. The considerations are reduced to a simple recognition of the facts. And the recognition is this: that Europe is subject to the absolute regime of banking capital.

We have seen a hostile attitude of French capital (not only French capital, as our readers will know, but we have decided to stick with the most obvious simplification) directed at a colonial enterprise of national character, ours in Tripolitania: we have seen a movement of French-European capital, repressive of the Balkan peoples' national motives. These Balkan peoples will succumb perhaps, because they are weak; we, much stronger, have run the risk of succumbing. However, we for Tripolitania, and the Balkan peoples for the reforms in Macedonia and for themselves, we have found ourselves faced with the same adversary who is either the Turk, as a good client protected by European plutocracy, or, reversing the terms, European plutocracy protecting the Turk, as a good client. And this is the entire system of the absolute plutocratic regime that Europe is subject to. The system of the Turk, of plutocracy, of the national rights that have been oppressed, or at the very least, taken hostage.

And this is the great evil of the historical European history that we are traversing. Our undertaking in Tripoli is of the best sort of all undertakings of conquest and colonization. It is an undertaking that meanwhile serves the national interests of a people, has the good fortune as well of being able to serve more general interests. We have found in Africa a territory that was *res nullius*, in that a people that possesses but do not produce is not a possessor; we will cultivate the territory, we will populate it, we will make it similar to other African colonies and other regions of Europe; and thus our undertaking, good for us, will be good for Europe itself, for the type [of person] that we will propagate in the desert, for civilization, for industry, for commerce, for the plutocracy itself finally, for all the activities of the human race. But we have run up against the plutocratic Europeo-Turkish system that is opposed to us for its immediate blind ends. The Balkan peoples are not decadent and inert Arab peoples; they are Christian peoples, of good stock, who already belong to the European family; and they are living, active, and productive peoples. And they are in a struggle with a half-dead, inactive, and unproductive enemy who holds their kinsmen under its rule, and they fight for themselves and for their kinsmen. But all their national, human, material and moral reasons come up against the same adversary: the plutocratic Europeo-Turkish system. We notice that the same old contests of territorial charac-

ter, however national in character they might be, are
of a higher moral character, the same old contests between state and state, over the division of the Turkish
empire, and we have taken a backseat before plutocracy's prevailment. Which, I repeat, is the great ig-
nominy and great evil of contemporary Europe. We
see, in short, that the moral motive, which must rule
the world, is made a slave to the plutocratic one,
which we do not say must be eliminated, but that it
must be subordinated.

We are beginning strongly to feel a need for
Europe to work for its own liberation. A growing
moral discomfort alerts us to this need. Europe finds
itself now, for the same politics, in a rather similar situation to that in which Italy found itself before occupying Tripolitania. Just as we felt, in the daily circulation of European politics, that our hands and feet were
bound by the unsolved problem of Tripolitania, Europe feels the same way now that it has no more freedom of movement to solve its own problems, thanks
to its having taken Turkey as a client, to be protected
and exploited as a client of plutocracy. We are beginning to feel the need for freedom which undoubtedly
will begin a new period in European history.

IX. Plutocracy's Satellites[23]

Our conquest of Tripolitania is, as I have written on multiple occasions, an undertaking of great moral beauty. It is one of those undertakings wherein the people who accomplish it, as they think of themselves and their affairs, think also of others and do others' affairs. In the mirror of history it will be seen how much the French, English, and Italians did, by conquering colonies on the African coast, for the future of European civilization which has world hegemony. First in order of time were the French and English, then the Italians. The merit of these last is in having reconnected, for European civilization, the east of Africa (English Egypt) with the west (French Tunisia, Algeria, and Morocco) by occupying the great, central Tripolitan swath of land. The Islamic empire has lost one of its three Mediterranean shores; it has lost one of its three continents. And the Asiatic adversary is as sterile as the European civilization is fecund. The life of the world, the economic and moral life, thrives under European civilization. Therefore, wherever it takes over from Islam, whether that be Turkish or Arabian Islam, it gives benefit to the world whose hegemony it possesses. This hegemony imposes duties on it: to provide and procreate. European civilization provides and procreates. And Italy, by attending strictly to its own affair this year, has taken part in so great a work. In the history [that we see unfolding be-

---

[23]Original footnote: November 1912.

fore our eyes], the actions of men and nations appear coordinated on a much vaster scale.

On that premise, the link that connects our conquest of Tripolitania with the war that the four Balkan allies wage against Turkey is quite clear. The two wars have the same extraordinary historical merit: also, the four allies make an effort to expel the sterile Asiatic adversary from one of the three continents, from Europe. Already expelled from Africa, it is being expelled from Europe, and in Asia itself there is a need to push back on it, to be able to develop the economic life of the world and the superior moral life on the three continents around the Mediterranean.

Now, what has happened, both for us and for the Balkan allies? What has happened is this: that in addition to having the same material enemy, the Turk, we had, and they still have, the same moral enemy. The enemy is the entirety of Europe, which the *statu quo* of the Ottoman empire stands in the middle of; the *statu quo* in which the old politics of national character and the new business of capitalistic character are consolidated, the first superimposed on the second, like one stratum on top of another in the earth. One might say that our and the Balkan allies' worst enemy was and is the international European financial and industrial plutocracy. You see what France is doing. Well, France represents the worsening of the industrial policy practiced by Germany in the Ottoman empire. Indeed, they say that the first traveling salesman of German manufacturers is the German emperor, but he is always and ever just an emperor who, if his immediate purpose was that of doing business for his aforementioned manufacturers, his mediate purpose is tending to the economy first, then to the political interests of his empire. By all indications, the politics of Wilhelm II in Asia Minor, being of an individual and industrial and financial and impresarial character today, being of an imperial character tomorrow, strives for a political conquest for the German empire, strives for a superior conquest: for the hegemony of German civilization in the world. Some writer has already noted it, and it is evident. But it is also evident that the France of French royalty, [represented] today in the person of Poincaré and company, republican, democratic, humanitarian France, the beacon and leader of all the ideals of the dreamers of ideals, France today is striving for naked and raw capital. First among the *plutocratic nations*, France is, or at least it has wanted to be, the coryphaeus of conferences and interventions in the Balkans, in favor of peace, in favor of Turkey, in short, and against the Balkan allies; for its own plutocracy, in short. In summary, we conclude that the two wars, the Balkan War and the Libyan War, *which, moreover, are the wars of nations of a proletarian character*, have had and have the same enemy: European plutocracy. European plutocracy has made itself the antagonist of undertakings of great moral beauty and of greater value for the history of Europe and the world. For those who understand, the two wars are wars of redemption. European plutocracy has been and is their antagonist.

The curious thing is that even socialist France acts similarly through pacifism. One of the most delicious pleasures for us these days is this: to hear so-

cialists shriek like wounded eagles against the war.
They do what plutocracy does. In other words, they
are the unwitting (their blindness hurts me, but it
needs to be said to save their face) – they are plutocracy's unwitting satellites. There is a proletarian who
should be dear to European socialism, and it is the
Macedonian farmer; and there was a proletarian who
ought not to have displeased it, and it was the Arab
farmer of Tripolitania. All those who understand the
broad and deep reasons of historical life know that
from the Balkan War and the Libyan War the human
redemption of either of these two proletariats can
emerge. But the proletariat's advocate, socialism, because it is for peace and against the war, acts as plutocracy's and Turkey's satellite, against the one and
the other proletariat, against the people and against
the wars from which the human redemption of the
one or the other can emerge. It is united with plutocracy through a doctrine. Which is, in theatrical jargon,
a "comical position." What, frankly, is more comical
than this socialism which, without realizing it, helps
that capital abroad which attempts to destroy it domestically? As soon as it realizes it, it would no
longer be comical, but criminal.

There is a socialist who, as our readers know,
is very popular in France, Italy, and the rest of Europe, and his name is Jean Jaurès. Now, it is very curious to see this leader of socialism want the same
thing for the Balkans that the plutocratic French republic's minister, Poincaré, wants, who, without a
doubt, is an agent of plutocratic French businesses:
peace, that is, and not war. Jean Jaurès has recently
shown his admiration for the "three peaceful nations,"

France, Germany, and England. Bravo! They are the *three plutocratic nations* par excellence. The leader of French socialism stands for them and against the war of redemption for *proletarian nations*. In its clamorous bosom, that riverbed of beastly assemblies, two currents, one socialist and the other plutocratic, on French soil naturally, join forces and the socialist hymn rises from the socialist leader of France to the three plutocratic nations. The organizer is peace. Which is precisely what is wanted for the plutocratic businesses' profit. Jean Jaurès is, in short, the natural socialist of the natural minister of contemporary France. This plutocratic-socialistic "comical position" embodied in one person is so very French.

And it is pointless to say that pure pacifism, bourgeois pacifism, would also play into plutocracy's hand if it could somehow play into it. We know that the many peaceful currents that pass through the European atmosphere are from a plutocratic source. Thus the three peaceful nations, France, Germany, and England are peaceful primarily because they are plutocratic. Finally, pacifism would want to erect an ideal perfection, like what it dreams of, above the reality of imperfections. By opposing the Libyan War and the Balkan War, bourgeois pacifism, like socialist pacifism, helps plutocracy maintain by means of the Turks the tyranny of injustice in Europe and the tyranny of sterility in Africa, which is the supreme injustice against eternal nature.

X. How Democracy Might Depopulate France[24]

A great French writer, Leroy-Beaulieu,[25] in a recently published book, *La question de la population* (Alcan), attributes the declining population in France for the most part to democratic ideas. He begins with this declaration: "The example of almost all civilizations, ancient and modern, leads, as will be shown by numerous proofs, to the conclusion that civilization, especially democratic civilization, tends, if not immediately, at least after a few generations, to depress the birth rate, and often to make it lower than the mortality rate, however low we might be able to bring that right now. By civilization we mean, in addition to the development of the city and that of the middle class, the almost universal propagation of ease, of instruction, of convenience, of individual and family ambitions, and the prospect available to everyone to climb the social ladder." More than twenty-five years ago the same Leroy-Beaulieu wrote: "The example of France and that part of the United States called New England, which lies on the Atlantic coast, seems to prove that at a certain level of prosperity and, with the inspiration of democratic sentiments, the tendency toward population growth becomes excessively weak."

By democracy must be understood here the

---

[24]Original footnote: Summer, 1913.

[25]Leroy-Beaulieu: Paul Leroy-Beaulieu (AD 1843-1916) French economist and author.

essence of democracy; one must have a sense of the profound which is lacking in newspaper *reporters* and men of parliament: we are at a point where changeable laws of society and politics intersect with the immutable laws of nature, and they are at odds.

Here then is what must be understood by democracy. First of all, what Leroy-Beaulieu expresses by a word that often comes up in his writing: *arrivism*. Individual and familial arrivism. Centuries of political policies led to this extreme democratic result, to individualize man in an extreme way and the concept that he has of life and the world around him. It has nothing to do here with that healthy individualism that everyone understands when individual energy, or the spirit of individual initiative, is discussed; it has to do with an unhealthy formation of the individual who has come to suppress in himself the reasons for collective life. The entirety of history lies between these two tendencies, the tendency to subordinate the individual to society, and the tendency to subordinate society to the individual; and by society we mean a particular sort of society, the national sort. The entirety of history over the last few centuries is explained by a progressive prevailment of the so-called rights of man over the rights of the nation, and ultimately, through liberalism, and in spite of the patriotic heroism of the French Revolution and the collective reaction of socialism, we have arrived at this democratic extreme, which by now is as much the triumph of the individual as it is the reaction that has risen against it, and at first there was the reaction of the class with socialism, whereas now there is the reaction of the vaster body [of society] that brings all the classes, the nation, together with nationalism.

With man individualized in the sense we have mentioned, here we are now at that individual and familial arrivism that Leroy-Beaulieu speaks about: man, in short, thinks only of himself and his closest friends or family, his children, and to hell with the rest of the world. And, in fact, Leroy-Beaulieu shows how France might perish because of French fathers' and mothers' arrivism.

It is a hedonistic arrivism. France in the last hundred years has accumulated, it is said, around 300 billion, and it closed its heroic period in the '70s before entering into its bourgeois, pacifistic, mercantile, plutocratic, and bureaucratic period. The French citizen's arrivism is like the historical period that France went through; it is bourgeois, pacifistic, mercantilistic, plutocratic, and bureaucratic. By reading Leroy-Beaulieu's book, it is seen how, for each one of these words that seem so general and foreign, French fathers and mothers, in the nocturnal intimacy of the bedroom, kill France by as little as one child, that famous third child that is necessary for increasing the population. They do that, in short, for their own prosperity and for that of their one offspring, two at most, for reasons of luxury and pleasure. French hedonistic arrivism has produced its feminine prototype: the woman who in order to preserve her beauty sterilizes the mother in her. In this respect, French literature, the novel, and theater are good educators. Leroy-Beaulieu's book is the ultimate condemnation of contemporary French civilization which we, uncouth Italian provincials, are the disciples of. And to certain among us it does not seem enough. Few notice the danger of a major spiritual contagion for Italy in the closer friendship with its Latin sister who is so much more progressive. Several months ago, in Rome, to a luminary of parliament, I made a comment that we are too much under the influence of French culture. The luminary replied: "And then? It's totally fine. Those French are so exquisite!" Which words remind me of those by Leroy-Beaulieu at the bottom of page 262 of his book:

> *Contemporary politicians at any level, from communal city councilors to ministers, are, in general, and with little exception, one of the most vile and mean-spirited bunch of sycophants and fawners ever known by humanity. Their only aim is to adulate basely and to promote all the popular prejudices that are also their own in a vague way, not having dedicated one instant of their life to reflection or observation.*

The individualized man is a man freed from the reasons of mystery. There are mysterious and very evident laws that rule the universal life of the species and cosmos. From this sea in which every being is like a drop of water, the individual is extracted, with all the knowledge in his brain. Just as we saw the woman sterilize the mother in herself, so the man has sterilized the divine in himself, and he is all brain now. Contemporary democratic individualism is also an extreme cerebralization of man who in turn cerebralizes all things. He cerebralizes the future of humanity in humanitarianism, pacifism, internationalism, and all the consimilar cerebral systematizations of the future that are so hateful to the man who is bound with instinctive forces that are perpetually and immutably active. In France, we have arrived at the *conscious generation*; and in Leroy-Beaulieu's book one sees how this extreme product of individual cerebralism kills France with that third child that is not born. While the statistics indicate that a certain moderate natality is maintained only in those French provinces where "ancient customs and traditional ideas" still survive: Brittany, Corsica, Alps, Lozère, and a few other provinces.

After which, what else must be meant by contemporary democracy? What must be meant is a legislation and a custom. And in Leroy-Beaulieu's book one can see how both, by indulging the *demos* too much, which is something that the French type of contemporary democracy consists in doing, finish by diminishing the *demos*. The numbers are alarming. French doctors affirm that 35% and even 40% of maternities are interrupted between the fourth and seventh month. Others affirm that at the present moment there are more abortions than births. In Paris, there would be 70 thousand abortions per year, compared to 63 thousand births. In France, there would be half a million abortions altogether, roughly two thirds the number of births. These numbers seem very high to Leroy-Beaulieu, especially for the countryside, but he must recognize along with physicians that the problem continues to worsen. According to a report by the "French Obstetrical Society," one third of conceptions are aborted in large cities; in the countryside much less; therefore, Leroy-Beaulieu calculated the annual number of children killed before birth to be somewhere around 100 thousand. And the problem is rapidly growing.

Well then, what does the public do about it? It does not bother itself. And the judiciary? It absolves. Democracy subordinates political power to the electorate, and every other power is subordinated. The tribunals serve as best they can, by absolving, and "the good judge," the flower of democracy's judiciary, rises in honor. In the general relaxation of powers and the public that results from it, the supreme perversion becomes codified. Leroy-Beaulieu's book in fact concludes with a ruling from the French court of cassation that declares that neo-Malthusian propaganda is unpunishable. And it wrecks havoc in France.

As Italians, we need to know all this in order to be careful ourselves. As we ascend, we must do all that we can so that our moral sanity is preserved for as long as possible. So that the historical period we are going through might last as long as possible. Our neighbors were in the same period, and for centuries and centuries they gave of themselves with as much generosity as no other people before them. And this is the great France that we must imitate and love.

Today, the Italian people, by proliferating, by crossing the sea, and by working on five continents, obey the sacred laws of life.

Above all, by acting to conquer what it must. The struggle between nations can sometimes be illuminated by comparing it to the struggle between the classes. But if we speak solely about the economic struggle, one does not understand. Among the peoples who surpass us today, we go forward to our conquest, with all our spiritual values and for all our spiritual values, in order to produce a civilization of our own that might transform the world.

We go at this very moment together with the five million workers that we have dispersed throughout the world, and with the hundreds of thousands of soldiers that already hold Africa. This is our sacred era, made by effort and struggle, in the profoundness of world history.

XI. On the Eastern Frontier[26]

A posthumous volume by Henry Houssaye, *La patrie guerrière*, informs us of a very important thing, which is this: from the second half of the last century to the present, the democratic malady of anti-militarism has so diminished that one can seriously foresee its proximate end. Even without calculating the beneficial effects of the most recent wars and international conflicts. Even before 1911, anti-militarism's time had run its course, although it might seem like the exact opposite in France where the fury of Hervé and the propaganda of the General Confederation of Labor have corrupted a large part of the army. There is one thing worse than anti-militaristic action and that is anti-militaristic ideology. The first is nothing more than a means of socialist action; the second is the effect and cause of the ruling classes' breakdown.

The French writer of whom we speak, in some of his pages against anti-militarism, gathers quotes by French deputies of the second empire. "Yes, gentlemen," exclaimed Jules Simon, "one thing alone makes the fatherland invincible, and that is freedom!" And Jules Fabre: "The most powerful nation is the one that can disarm: and for that reason, instead of building up our forces, we are heading towards disarmament." And Garnier Pagès: "The time for standing armies, mountains, and rivers is past. The true frontier is patriotism. The levy in mass is good enough." And

[26]Original footnote: Summer, 1913.

even Jules Simon: "We want an army of citizens, not soldiers, an army that is invincible at home and disarmed to lead the war without. Militarism is the plague of the era. There is no army without a military spirit, we are told. Well then, in that case, we want an army that is not an army."

Similar stupidities are not repeated today in any parliament; a sign that national consciousness has everywhere been growing sane again.

Houssaye's book has this merit especially: it belongs to that restorative literature that is now being brought out in France by multiple publishers. They are the organic forces of that very noble people who attempt to regain the upper hand on socialism, demagogy, crazy humanitarianism, internationalism, pacifism, all dissolving forces. *La patrie guerrière* is the old France, it is the old heroic Celtic-Napoleonic spirit that wants to rise up again in new generations.

The book by this famous historian of Napoleon is very Celtic, very Napoleonic. There is a care of souls executed in the most ingenuous way, in precisely the same way one might speak to simple souls. Houssaye delivers a panegyric of the soldiers of France beginning with the greatest of them all, Napoleon, and then continuing with Alexandre Dumas Davy, Cambronne, Berthier, the corsair Surcouf, others from other times. The French emphasis, and we know it well, is not lacking. There is, for example, a description of the infantry charge, not a historical charge, but a general description of the infantry charge which in Italian is inconceivable and not even possible in the language of the Romans who were so warlike, and not even in German perhaps, nor in any classical language. The description of the charge is not so much to instruct as it is to arouse enthusiasm, the frenzied description of the formal charge is pure French, or rather Celtic, whereas [as Italians] we can conceive only of the narration of a charge, which is the equivalent of action. And yet, this emphasis, this rhetoric even, we might say, is an endearing quality of the French who have been a people of such ardor and energy. The ardor of their words in literature appears to us like an effulgence of their acts throughout history.

Nevertheless, it is well not to pass in silence over similar French literature which is a moral document in addition to a political one, in addition to the government's law that attempts to reform the nation, the army. We are accustomed to turning to the joyful and pleasure-loving France; we ask for pleasure from France, in their novels, theater, champagne, fashion, and prostitutes. On the other hand, we are familiar with the democratic and republican France, Jacobin France, the *nation-lumière*, the France of Combes and of Jean Jaurès, first charlatan of France, just as Baiardo was the first cavaliere. But there is a new France, much more important today, at this moment in time, and it is the tragic France that is striving to reform itself. It is precisely in literature and on a small scale the France of the *patrie guerrière*, and it is, in politics and on a large scale, the France of converted socialists, of the law of the three-year draft. This tragic France, to all peoples of the world, but to us first because we are the closest, can give and gives small and big lessons. And this is the France we must look to from now on.

Who does not know about the decline in the French birthrate? But one must also know, for example, that the three-year draft is a castigation. It is a tragic thing that is happening between French individuals and the French nation. The individuals reduce the number of children they have. It is the effect of vices, the effect primarily of hedonistic, individualistic materialism. French families, the father and mother in their bedrooms, in the nocturnal vigils of their bedrooms, wound the French nation in its preservation. They no longer have one of those feelings that encourage men to build societies, to make nations, peoples, lineages, species, and they have one desire only, their own personal prosperity and the prosperity of their children when they become adults. And therefore, so as not to have too many mouths to feed, every now and then they kill the nation by not having a child. And the nation could dwindle in inhabitants and little by little be extinguished. But it *must* be preserved, it has the will to be preserved, or better still: to become larger and more powerful. Someone encourages it in that. Who is this someone? The French in their language call him the *Allemand*.[27] And against this German which has many soldiers, France must have many soldiers; but not having enough children they must extend the length of the draft. And thus, French individuals are, for their egoism, punished, in themselves and in their children, with a major burden. They must give back to the nation what they have taken from the nation. But who is the *Allemand*? Evidently, underneath this individual of another lineage,

---

[27]*Allemand*: French for "German."

underneath this French word, there is the mysterious will that has assigned to nations, to nations and their wars, a task for its purpose. This conscious will that makes the history of humanity what it is, we can imagine it in no other way, it has pitted a Frenchman against a German, and the Frenchman, like the German, must be ready. It was no longer his fault, he must recuperate through his castigation. This castigation, as we said, is the law of the three-year draft.

Do we still have time? The *patrie guerrière,* having been awakened with a start, does it still have time to save the fatherland? Now is the tragic moment. Germany continues to grow; previously it had more than half a million soldiers, now it has almost one million, with the possibility that it can have a million and a half tomorrow, without effort. Over there the bedroom by and large supplies the caserne. But in France, after the three-year draft, what will happen? What law of the state, what incitement, what reward will overcome the sterility in the bedroom, will overcome materialism and hedonism? Or must everything be done for the caserne and to hell with the bedroom? The three-year draft will be extended to four years and so forth? Is that possible? Or will France give up the terrible fight?

Nevertheless, today, France's best friend is Germany. France has other friends and allies, but none like Germany, because none excites it to moral action like Germany does. England is a friend, and Russia is an ally, but Germany is the most efficacious ethnic tonic. Fear of the German stimulates in the French nation the instinct of its conservation and acts like an organic force, against socialism, demagogy, humanitarianism, proletarian and financial internationalism, pacifism, anti-militarism in short, all the dissolving forces. Who is it really that awakens the *patrie guerrière*? The German soldier. It is the German soldier who, sounding the reveille of terrible war across the Rhine, awakens French spirituality against materialism, awakens French altruism against individualism, awakens the French sense of duty against the feeling of pleasure.

And the amount of force that is thus manifested is contained in the law of the nation. In the nation exposed to antagonisms with other nations.

Towards the end of Henry Houssaye's book, there are some magnificent pages on the garrisons in the east:

> *No distraction there, no worldly pleasure. Always work, the conscripts' instruction, school, exercise, target practice, long marches, field duty. In such an active existence in which every hour is occupied, a soldier has no time to think about the well-being that he is lacking, about the world of pleasures he is exiled from. And even if he thought about them, he would not miss them. Those officers create for themselves a higher conception of life. Constrained, dominated by the army and by the duties of the military profession, every day they love it with more passion, because every day in*

*the vicinity of the frontier they better
understand the utility and feel the
greatness of it. And just as it is for the
officers so is it for the soldiers. When
these latter have had enough instruction and are able to appreciate the
greatness of the lesson, they are sent
out into the woods and, their maneu-
ver finished, they stand back at the
embankment and shout "Lorraine!"
Then there is a moment of silence, a
solemn, serious, and meditative moment that all of a sudden seems to grip
the heart and stop the breath. At that
moment it seems that officials and soldiers possess nothing but a devotion,
the fatherland, and a united heart and
a united soul directed at the unwaver-
ing goal. And there was no need for
great moral theories to be put forward
at this point: it was enough for the
men to gaze.*

One gets the feeling of an extraordinary moral
strength in these pages. The locations, there by the
German border, are purifying, fortifying. There is a
religious atmosphere there, as if in a temple when the
rites are performed.

XII. The Morality of Productive Possession[28]

A book by Corrado Gini, professor at the University of Padua, *Demographic Factors of the Evolution of Nations*,[29] recently published by Bocca of Turin, demonstrates how there might be a general law of depopulation by individuals, classes, and nations.

"People," Gini writes, "collocated higher up on the social scale, those who make up the upper classes, generally have a reproductivity rather weaker than the people who make up the so-called lower strata of the population."

The same goes, naturally, for classes.

The same goes for nations.

Regarding individuals, in addition to other evidence, there is that furnished by the fiscal statistics of successions. In France, an annual median of 358,000 property owners who pass away leave behind 285,000 children.

Property owners, therefore, in France tend to disappear. In Italy, instead, 100 property owners leave behind 114 children, but the general population, in the period from 1874 to 1909, is calculated to have left behind from 100 to 134 [percent more]. So, even in

---

[28]Original footnote: February 1914.

[29]*Demographic Factors...*: *I fattori demografici dell'evoluzione delle nazioni,* Fratelli Bocca, Turin, 1912.

Italy, property owners produce less offspring than non-property owners.

And the more they possess, the less offspring they produce.

> *In Italy (1892/93-1893/94), direct-line succession constituted 87% of successions under 500 lire; in those between 500 and 5,000 lire, they drop to 75% and do not represent but 72% in those above 5,000 lire. In France (1898), the median amount of inheritance was much higher relative to the lower number of surviving children: from 9,000 lire, when the deceased left more than six children, it reached almost 14,000 when the surviving children were only two. When there are, then, no children at all among the heirs, the median amount of inheritance rises to as high as 21,500 lire.*

The same is found elsewhere.

And the same law holds true with respect to professionals: the higher one climbs the work ladder, from manual laborers to intellectuals, the less children that are produced: manual laborers proliferate more than clerks or professionals. Professional and economic conditions go hand in hand. And we observe this: manual laborers, clerks, and professionals, the less they proliferate, the more they earn.

The general law, then, is this: men, the higher they climb the social ladder both economically and morally, the more they tend to disappear.

The same goes for families.

The same goes for classes.

So, as the upper classes continually tend to disappear because of wealth and culture, what must happen? What must happen is that from the bottom rung of society, from the poor and ignorant classes, continuous replacements must be provided. A continuous column, so to speak, of humanity rises from the fresh working classes to replenish the seignorial classes that are becoming exhausted.

Which explains certain historic phenomena, such as, for example, the diffusion of Christianity. Having been the religion of the lowest class, how did it succeed in becoming the religion of the vast majority? Not only by its force of conquest, but also because the "lower classes that had embraced such beliefs were headed to become the great majority of the population." The same fact explains how in many regions where dominated peoples and dominant peoples lived, the anthropological characteristics of the former remain while those of the latter have disappeared. Gini writes the following:

> *Cimbri, Heruli, Goths, Rugi, Turcilingi, Alamanni, Saxons, Lombards, Franks, all representatives of the blond dolichocephalic peoples of the north, invaded the beautiful regions of northern Italy during the historical period, preceded most probably by related populations during the prehistoric*

*period, and naturally more or less
tended to gravitate around Milan
where the various transalpine passes
converge. Well, I find a homogeneity
of the cephalic index there, an indica-
tion of racial unity, such as is encoun-
tered in the heart of the Rhaetic and
Lepontic Alps, the undisturbed mil-
lenarian seat of Aryan populations.*

On the contrary, in Sardinia, which is extolled
"as the land where the race of the primitive inhabitants of Italy remains intact," what did the same professor from the University of Padua find? He found
"a nucleus of populations notably heterogeneous in
their cephalic index, which would suggest a mixture,
or juxtaposition of more or less diverse ethnic elements." What is the explanation? An abundant importation, especially from the XIV to the XVII century,
of Berber, Arab, Turkish, and Tartar slaves. "It is
quite probable that in terms of numbers those heterogeneous ethnic elements ought not to exceed those remaining through the centuries on the plains of Lom-
bardy, but they were differentiated in quality: the former belonged to ruling classes and they vanished into
thin air, whereas the latter made up the lowest classes
and remained stable and proliferated with a vitality
that even today we can appreciate the effects of.

The ruling classes consequently would have
vanished without "the demographic substitution" of
the lower classes for the upper.

Now, the readers know what is happening in
France. The population of France, with the exception

of a few provinces, is dropping nationally. That happens for the same reasons that the classes of greater wealth and culture *dwindle in population*; because France is, on a global scale, also an upper *class* in terms of wealth and culture, in terms of the civilization it has achieved effectively. And such a comparison, with respect to the same demographic effects, between nations and classes, is extremely important.

But the importance increases when one knows this second fact: that France, becoming demographically impoverished, is also becoming economically impoverished. France loses wealth because it loses energy in industries and tends to diminish industries, because it loses energy in commerce and tends to diminish commerce, because it depreciates its own land.

> *The net income from rural property resulted in 2,645 million in 1879 according to the official survey; 2,581 in 1884; 2,368 in 1892; in 1895 it was valued (Coste) at only 2 billion; in 1908 (Caillaux) at no more than 1,760 million; in thirty years then a 33% reduction. To the reduction of income corresponds a reduction of the land value; this is actually much more serious because agricultural crises have lowered the value of real estate investments: from 91 and a half billion in 1880, the land value had dropped to 79 billion in 1890, and to no more than 64 billion between 1900 and*

1905; a reduction of almost 30% in about twenty-three years. Such reduction is realized in the lands of all classes and all crops.

And that there is the proof that in France a cause and effect relationship exists between depopulation and impoverishment. I cite from Gini's book again:

It is to the drop in the birthrate, insufficient to address the movements of people out of the countryside and into the city, as happens in other nations, that the shortage of hands *in agriculture is due. From there, the forced shift in crops, the increase in wages, the reduction of profit and land value. The stagnation in the number of consumers is responsible for the crises of overproduction in those industries whose market is predominantly national. Entrepreneurs say that they are forced to keep in hire the more deficient and troublesome employees because of the scarcity of workers which prevents a rigorous selection. One of the circumstances that makes workers more likely to engage and persist in strikes is the lack, or scarcity, of offspring. And the active social exchange deriving from an unequal reduction in the birthrate is one of the causes of the progressive concentration of wealth. A correlation between an increase in the population and an increase in international commerce has also been demonstrated.*

But here is the proof that resolves the matter once and for all: in those departments where the population has grown, the annual number of successions has also grown: whereas in those departments where the population has dropped, it has dropped.

Here then is the law: when men acquire property and riches, they tend to lose productive energy, and when they lose productive energy, they tend to lose property and riches. This biological-economic relationship is a constant, it is demonstrated by ancient history as well as by contemporary history, and by the history of all peoples, as well as by the history of one people alone. The law therefore is a constant, which shows itself to be natural. Nothing is more manifest than that it is natural for a man first to strive to acquire property and wealth and then, after having obtained them, to tend to favor repose and transform them into his enjoyment. In other words, to deform himself and his possessions and riches. And in the act of deformation, the man loses energy; and his possessions and riches, land, industry, commerce, all lose productivity. It is as if nature strikes whoever has violated its laws in order to punish him, and his possessions and riches are taken away from him – as with the man, so too with the class, the people, the nation, the empire, for which reason they begin to grow unproductive, in other words, they lose their proper function, and they draw near to others whose virtue can turn them around so as to reacquire their proper function, which is to produce. This is it exactly. In France, as the population drops, and as its monetary wealth – not yet apparent today, but it will be tomorrow – and the value of its real estate tends to drop, the consumption of foodstuffs and clothing rises, "the theater receipts and the size of gambling bets grow ever larger." Enjoyment. Man has become a parasite of the wealth that originally he was the producer of. In French savings accounts there is a lot of money that *just sits there*, no longer put to work in industry or taking risks. Ethnic diminution, that is, of energy and courage. A French writer cited by Gini grumbles accordingly:

> *Our national temperament used to be bold, confident, adventurous. The French were chivalrous, liberal, and magnanimous. Seeing them now, it is as though their characteristics have changed. Who would recognize today in the triumphant bourgeoisie, in whom the entire nation seems to be embodied, the heirs of the crusaders, the fearless colonizers of the 17th century, the soldiers of the Revolution and the empire? The French bourgeoisie* has reduced the national soul *to the size of its conceptions. It possesses the prudence of the small shopkeeper at the same time as the narrow-mindedness of the worker, the timidity of the ancient servant, something of the ancient persecuted sects as well... The*

economy has been transformed into parsimony, and the focus on savings is starting to look like avarice. *And a bourgeois father does not arrange for his children any better than he invests his money: provided he gains a little interest thereby, he is happy; and similarly, provided his children have* a secure position, *or so it is believed, however low it might be, he considers himself satisfied.*

In short, Frenchmen and money *are coasting.*

Readers understand that the biological-economical law is transformed into a moral law. According to nature's indications, a moral relationship is established between the possessor and the possession. It is a relationship of productivity. In short, when the possessor, whether a man, his family, the nation, the empire, makes the possession produce, a moral relationship exists between them. On the other hand, [when the possession is not made to produce,] an immoral relationship exists. Productivity, moral relationship; improductivity, immoral relationship. A sterile population destroys as much humanity as it creates. An inert possessor destroys as much land as he occupies by not making it produce. And there is a law against destroyers.

On that rests the morality of imperialism.

That "demographic replacement" that must occur from the lower to the upper classes, lest the productive energy in a people is not replenished, must also happen from nation to nation, lest the productive energy in the world is not replenished. It happens as a result of imperialism. Which, ultimately, is nature's categorical imperative for the conservation and propagation of the species and its production.

The same law of necessary replacement condemns socialism. It justifies it as a class struggle which indeed corresponds to the replacement, but condemns it as a definitive arrangement of society. A society of equals excludes the replacement and thus excludes its own continuation. Only among social differences does the replacement act as a replenisher.

Among social differences and ethnic differences.

And this, therefore, is our moral, general, and fundamental law.

It is the principle of all our politics, foreign and domestic.

XIII. New National Doctrines and Spiritual Renewal[30]

This evening, o ladies and gentlemen, I propose to speak to you about the most important and delicate matter that has happened in the Italian soul in the last fifteen years.

The latest manifestation of this matter was heard throughout the world, it was a war of conquest; but the cause was intimate, and intimately in the Italian soul it unfolded year after year, in contemplative silence. I am certain that you, citizens of Trieste, will listen to me attentively.

I will speak to you simply, and to the point, as happens when one speaks about august and sacred things, because such is this Italian matter that I need to speak with you about. I am certain that you, citizens of Trieste, you especially, will listen to me with loving intelligence.

Now, what is this matter?

What are, in Italy, the new national doctrines?

When and how were the new national doctrines born?

There is no doubt that they were born in reac-

---

[30]Original footnote: A discourse given in Trieste on the evening of December 11, 1913, and in Fiume two evenings later.

tion to socialism.

While in France they were born in reaction to
the new regime, which had suppressed the old regime,
or at least in reaction to the politics of the new
regime; in Italy they were born in reaction to socialism, and that is enough to differentiate the new national doctrines of Italy since their origins, from the
new national doctrines of France.

What is socialism?

It is simply, gentlemen, a theoretical and practical construction of global imperialism, founded on a
event of historical reality that is incomparably small.
The historical reality – the industrial transformation
of the XIX century, that is – gave major importance
to the working proletariat, and consequently that proletariat had a momentum encouraging it to occupy a
higher economic and political place in the class hierarchy. Add socialism to that mix, which is of a messianic and demagogic, even if Marxist, character, and
it imparts the idea of an unlimited illusion to the momentum of historical reality: it signals that the goal of
proletarian conquest is world domination.

The evolutionary process, so to speak, from
the historical reality that allots to the working class
only a higher place, to socialism which allots to it the
dominion of the world, is as follows. The proletariat's
adversary is the bourgeoisie; but this is not a society
in and of itself: just as the proletariat is a class, so too
the bourgeoisie is a class; that is, both the bourgeoisie
and the proletariat are two minor organisms making
up, as parts, a larger organism. The larger organism is

in fact the nation. Thus, socialism sees the struggle between these two groups, the proletariat and the bourgeoisie, within one nation, as we said; and in this it rouses a true and proper revolution, by attempting to overturn two positions, that of the bourgeoisie and that of the proletariat. Socialism raises a revolution in the nation, and it evolved from striking at the bourgeoisie to striking at the nation, it evolved from a plan of doing the greatest possible harm to the bourgeoise to doing the greatest possible harm to the nation. To attain such a goal, it attempted to transcend the concept of nation with the traditional concept of internationalism, redefined in economic terms. Nations, the well-known borders, had no more need to exist; these old terrestrial, ethnic, historical entities were no longer entities, and the only entities that existed, constructed on a solid commonality of economic interests, were the two classes, uninterruptedly extended throughout the world and put in opposition – the proletariat and the bourgeoisie. Thus, with nations destroyed, what remained was the world; with the bourgeoisie destroyed, what remained was the dominion of the proletariat. And thus, messianic and demagogic socialism, with the class struggle and class-based internationalism, achieved its dream, a first in history, of a class-based global imperialism.

In simple terms, o ladies and gentlemen, socialism did much harm to the nation, by revolutionizing it internally in its unity and suppressing it externally in its individuality. It had gotten to the point where it was unclear anymore which one socialism hated more: the part, the bourgeoisie, or the whole, the nation; whether it was aiming to wipe from the face of the earth the former, or the latter. And this lasted for many years. It is superfluous to add that during all that time the very love of the nation languished, and national consciousness grew dim.

But national consciousness was not spent, it continued to exist as a small flame in a few men. There was a grief in them, there was a kind of disorientation, a dismay, an emptiness in their life. And whatever fortune they had in their life as men, whatever their day was like between common pleasures and displeasures, that emptiness, that dismay, that disorientation, that grief, like a domestic tragedy, never left them. And their tragedy was truly a domestic one because the whole that they belonged to like small particles was domestic in their heart; and that great entity that went by the name of the fatherland was domestic in their small being. When the socialist scourge turned it upside down, those men became aggrieved. For many years, they lived in prey to a tragic pathos that they alone knew.

That pathos was the beginning of new national doctrines.

In the beginning, they were none other than true and proper reactions of the instinct of self-preservation which nations have, just like individuals. The nation's instinct of self-preservation, menaced by socialism, spoke to those men who had a more developed, more profound, stronger national consciousness.

The new national doctrines were, in essence, in the beginning, patriotism's cry of grief, and then they progressed into being an awareness of national means, a doctrine, systems of thought and action, in opposition to socialism, in order to defend the nation and make the nation triumph against socialism's assault on it, domestically in its unity with the class struggle, externally in its individuality with class-based internationalism. In order to defend the nation and make it emerge triumphant from the war that socialism was waging on it, with its intent to embody the dream of class-based global imperialism. Socialism had essentially initiated a new historical period, and in it the new national doctrines stood before it like antagonists, with the intent of breathing new life into a new historical period in which the old, indestructible, immutable, eternal principle of the nation, while the latest proposal of a class-based imperialism had been struck down, having arisen from the union of the class struggle and traditional internationalism; in which finally the principle of a nation, with its enemies defeated, could show new manifestations in the world, and in Europe, and in Italy, and coming out of Italy.

But as you know, o ladies and gentlemen, socialism was then what it has always been: it was materialistic. Socialism is an apex of materialism. It is materialism at the highest degree of individual and social saturation. The philosophy of the last few centuries, the same anti-Catholicism of the French Revolution, the discoveries and applications of contemporaneous physical sciences were converging to produce the same effect: man was no longer recognizable except by his materiality, and he no longer recognized the world except in its materiality. The dream of socialist imperialism was as vast as the world, but that vastness was in proportion to the narrowness and materialistic baseness of the economic law on which it was conceived. The class struggle, in a word, philosophism, the same beneficent science, the decadence of European civilization, the deviation of every culture, they were both the causes and the effects of a general materialism that no one and nothing escaped. Socialism was the triumph of materialism in the doctrines of human societies.

It is understandable, therefore, and it must be excused, if the new national doctrines were, at their origins, materialistic too; if they too hinted at forming a content of economic prevalence.

At certain moments, and several early on, they took initial shape in the form of a search for the means of a defense of the bourgeoisie. Evolving from there, they arrived at the conception of a national imperialism, a dominion, that is, an actual nation of foreign territories, productive colonial types, centers of trade, emigration, and so on. The traditional imperialism of nations was counterposed to the very new socialist, class-based imperialism.

But meanwhile the personality of the nation has reappeared, and it consists in its internal unity and in its external individuality; it has reappeared before us, before all those who, in their support, oppose ideas and actions to the ideas and actions of its adversary, socialism. Its organic unity has reemerged as the natural antithesis to the class struggle, its organic individuality has reemerged as the natural antithesis to internationalism and class-based imperialism. The personality of the nation, living and working in the world, has reemerged in the same programs of colonial occupations for the possession of commercial and emigratory outlets.

At this point, let us go back and review the first light of the spirit.

In what way?

In the simplest way. Furiously attacked by socialism, the nation re-presents its unity and its individuality in the passing moment; from this we are led to see it again in its continuity through the centuries. Such a continuity is not, and cannot be, anything but spiritual in nature. So the nation returns to being, before our very mind's eye, spiritual in nature.

From this point, the new national doctrines move past the historical period in which they arose, and they begin a new period. Materialism has ceased, spiritualism has begun again.

The nation stands before us like a spiritual fact, surrounded by the greatest moral values.

These values are all summarized in one: the idea of sacrifice which replaces the idea of utility. Whatever you might ask of the individual from his brief existence, for the nation that persists across the centuries and millennia, it is quite probable that the individual is a thing of sacrifice.

We must give socialism its due. As we said, and as you knew, ladies and gentlemen, socialism is materialistic. But, in the very act of reaching the height of materialism, it too, it too looks at things

from the opposite viewpoint. Meaning that socialism
finds the bourgeoisie in a state of extreme individualism, and from this state of advanced decadence it rises again to an earlier form of association, and creates
the class. History will need to take account of it.

But look: no matter how much socialism
wants to transform the world, that is, to go the maximum distance, it does not influence its followers except by the prospect of an immediate gain: the strike,
in order to increase wages. And this is one of the reasons that we can be certain that socialism will not
transform the world. Look at a socialist proletarian.
Does he have the class spirit, a certain spirit of sacrifice? Even if he had, socialism spoils it; even if he
were naturally disposed to have it, socialism does not
give him the time to mold it and make it his own, because it only engages him in strikes in order to increase his wages. Look at an assembly of socialist
workers when the secretary of the labor union makes
it vote on a motion for the continuation of a strike "to
the end." It is enthusiasm. But there is the prospect of
an increase in wages. As much to say, there is a great
deal of natural popular generosity spoiled by socialism. In everything that it does, socialism is what you
know, ladies and gentlemen; it is that school that you
know, of egotistical intent, of ingenerosity. It is so
much so that, by restricting all and sundry of its followers for the mere speculation of their wages, it succeeds in isolating them from the rest of the world: it
isolates them from other classes, it isolates them from
the nation, it isolates them from humanity, it isolates
them from the aims of civilization, as has been seen
in our Libyan War. Against which, during elections,

in the city and in the countryside, the socialist candidates incited the Italian people to revolt, to shed their blood and their money, not realizing that in this way, by dehumanizing themselves and dehumanizing by so much moralization of ingenerosity and cowardice, they severed every bond, not only between the Italian people and Italy, but also between the Italian people and the civilization that is worth this war and will be worth it in order to return finally to a continent that has been abandoned for one thousand five hundred years. And I really do not know anything more inhuman, more painful, and more horrendous, more tragic, than this solitude that socialism inflicts on the poor people in the world who have fallen under its spell.

Now, if you want to see what the spirit of sacrifice is like, put a socialist next to the highest creation of the spirit of sacrifice, which is the work of the nation. Put a socialist next to the soldier.

There is in history a prototype of the soldier – that of the French Revolution. They had managed to instill in him the consciousness of revolutionary ideas and of the idea of the fatherland which had become one. For this idea, that soldier went forward into battle, to die on all the fields of Europe, and there was nothing in it for him personally. He went to die for the one thing that existed for him in this idea: his enthusiasm. No other recompense, not on this earth, not in heaven. And this is, o gentlemen, without any doubt, one of the principle reasons that the French Revolution has had such a profound influence on the world. It is the soldier's reason.

For this is how it is: the less we act for ourselves, the more possibility we have to act for others, from a distance. And moral values, the more moral they are, the more force they have to act, to operate, to transform, to produce, to create from a distance, in the vastness of time and space. And the greater this vastness, the more moral the values are. Often, in Libya, in the depths of the oasis and on the sands of the desert, I saw our soldiers die. Nothing was left of them except a stiff trunk. They had given everything they had, and at twenty years of age they were dead without offspring. But seeing their blood spilt on the ground, it seemed to me that the ground was fecundated by them, and my mind, looking into the future, saw those places teeming with an Italian population of millions and millions of souls who were enjoying the richness of that land. So those young men had not begotten offspring, but the virtue of their blood had been carried far and bore fruit along the same paths as our first mother, the earth.

Without this force which moral values have, to suscitate life from a distance, the world, the entire world of men and their works would remain sterile in the course of one generation.

And behold: the new national doctrines have arisen precisely to re-examine the moral values contained in the concept of the nation.

And to shine a light on the first of those values, which is the idea of sacrifice.

And to re-establish, once and for all, the truth that the nation is of a spiritual nature.

The new national doctrines are a sociology

and a morality. As a sociology of national society, they study its essence, and recognize its spirituality; and as a morality, they derive moral values from that same spirituality.

Which are of two types.

First type: the part is subordinated to the whole; in other words, the individual is subordinated to the nation; or rather, the individual transcends himself in the nation.

And therefore, the idea of sacrifice instead of profit.

Duty instead of exigence.

Respect for hierarchy instead of anarchy.

Discipline instead of agitation.

The nation is considered the means to individual perfection.

Second type of moral values: The nation transcends itself in something that is greater than itself: in the concept of civilization.

The nation continually transcends itself, aiming to create its civilization, which is the supreme fruit, the supreme flower of its entire history, of its entire effort through the centuries, what our Roman forefathers summed up in two words, when, sensing all the fatigue and all the sanctity of their work, which still endures after two millennia and still renews itself – when they said this about themselves: "*Facere et pati fortia romanum est.*"[31] To act, and to endure.

And finally the nation considers the formation of its own civilization as a contribution to be made to the universal civilization of humanity. And this is the supreme transcendence, as much to say the supreme moral law.

That is, for the new doctrines that we are discussing, the nation is a means to the perfection of a great society of men over a long succession of centuries, and it is a means to the perfection of the world.

It is the greatest means, by size and strength.

You know, o ladies and gentlemen, that there are some universal ideals that are handed down from century to century and passed from people to people. There are certain ideas of justice, brotherhood, order, peace for all humankind. Well, of the new doctrines that we are discussing, in their final exposition, they have to do with the nation, have to do with nations as the means, as the instruments to bring reality ever closer to those ideas, to those ideals that are always blazing a new trail that is endless to human sight.

In other words, nations are the greatest force possible for instilling morality in the world.

So sovereign an event as the moralization of the world is never static and peaceful for new doctrines, not even in the most distant future, but it is continually and endlessly dynamic and agonistic. It is,

---

[31]*Facere et pati...*: Latin for "To do and to endure valiantly is the Roman way." Livy, *History of Rome*, 2.12 (Benjamin Oliver Foster).

that is, the nature of its strength that it does not refuse its task which is to fight and conquer in order to renew and create life and to impose and sustain order. It is, essentially, the nature of morality that is identified, as we have said, with the agonistic dynamism that never stops transforming the world, and by transforming it, it preserves it.

And behold, o gentlemen, the essence of the argument that you were kind enough to come here this evening to hear me speak on. And I am certain that to the degree that I have summarily exposed it to you, it has appeared to you for what it is: the most important event of the historical period that we are going through. We cannot think differently about this resurrection of spirituality in politics, we cannot think differently about this need for a moral renewal that we begin to feel, through politics.

There was no longer a political landscape in any direction that was not by now devoid of this flower; that was not by now empty of any spiritual content, or any moral content. Not one political thought, not one doctrine, not one action, not one party even.

In order to find something similar in that epoch, one must go back to socialism again, when at its first emergence it was met with so much generosity, so much illusion, so much youthfulness, so much ingenuousness, so much need for the faith and enthusiasm that is contained in the human heart. Socialism seemed so beautiful at that time, because of the human beauty that, being thirsty, it had gathered around it.

But having turned to face its stark reality, we saw it for what it was.

And then, across the entire spectrum of its political landscape, every glimmer of ideality was spent, every flame of love was spent, every religious sentiment in the lives of men and the nation was finished, every vastness of vision over their destinies was finished. No party, no doctrine, perhaps no politician, retained any memory of it.

When the new national doctrines suddenly emerged to effect what we have seen. A real and proper revolution in contemporary politics.

Their nobility resides in the truth that they spread; their fortune, in responding to a historical necessity.

Ladies and gentlemen.

Being at the end of my discourse now, perhaps you will be curious to ask me: Will our refined and perfected spirit perchance want to go further in the study of new doctrines? This moral perfectionment conceived of as a ladder of transcendence, of the individual in the class, the class in the nation, the nation in civilization, civilization in humanity, having arrived at the goal, will it lead us to cast our eyes on high? The new national doctrines, in short, after having arrived at their apex, will they make a small opening through which we can turn and see what once were called "the disquieting problems of the beyond"? Will it come to pass then, this event, new in history, that the nation might teach us to seek God?

The question is asked, but we are unable to respond. We feel only the perturbation and anxiety that it generates in our heart.

But if that were the case, it would have all the more demonstrated the loftiness of the political thought that I have had the honor of presenting to you, this evening, o ladies and gentlemen.

Man is so small and humble a being that he sees little and knows little of the world around him, and little of the laws that govern the world, and nothing of the higher causes, or the higher cause, which determined those laws. We are bound in mystery.

But there are some truths, some doctrines, some thoughts, some facts of man himself, which resemble the mountains which, for as low as they stand, seem to touch the sky, and seem like the radiant altar of the sun when it rises, to those who stand in the valley below. So man does and thinks things that are to him like the height of heights, when he sees the appearance of what must be above him, and a glimmer of its light.

It is wonderful that something like this has happened in politics.

And it is for me a source of pride and joy that this has happened in Italian politics, because it possesses such potential and such fecundity that Italy can effect a transformation of Italian stamp on the consciousness of other nations.

Citizens of Trieste! Several years ago, when the new national doctrines were approaching public consciousness in Italy, I first spoke about them to you, to you before others. At that time, I spoke about emigration, colonies, imperialism. Today, I wanted to return in order to tell you where we stand now, at this moment when those doctrines, after having taken some action and having had some good success, are laying the first foundations of one of those moral, ideal constructions that can turn a nation into a leader of world history.

XIV. Commemoration of the Battle of Adwa[32]

Invited to commemorate our fallen soldiers on this eighteenth anniversary of the Battle of Adwa, I think that one can do no better than to recount their extraordinary fate: how, that is, they fell in the saddest way only to rise again in the most fortunate way.

For years and years, we knew only of their very sad end, and only now do we know also of their happy resurrection.

Their fate was equal to that of the man for whose plan their twenty-year-old lives had been cut down in the Adwa valley: with whom they died, with whom they rose again.

Their fate was equal to that of the nation for which they had fought and had not won: having died with the nation, with the nation they rose again.

To the effect that our commemoration, o citizens of Bologna, will be twofold: more sorrowful in the first part, more exultant in the second. After days of suffering, we too will launch our cry: Cheer up hearts! Our dead have risen! The soldiers, the man, the nation, have risen.

To be honest, whoever lived through those days, as an Italian, as a man, that March 2, when the news of the defeat arrived, that March 5, when

---

[32]Original footnote: Discourse given in Bologna, at the Teatro del Corso, March 1, 1914.

Francesco Crispi announced his resignation from the government; whoever was alive on that day of disgraceful peace and in the years that followed, knew a new sort of compassion: the compassion for so many thousands of young men dead for the fatherland, pointlessly.

Their compatriots of thirty years earlier had not died like this on the fields of Custoza or at sea near Lissa; not as unfortunate, although they too lay down without victory; but not as unfortunate, because they were leaving someone behind to continue the work in which they had lost their life: they left all the people of Italy, its men and its king, to continue the work of the independence and unification of Italy; whereas those who died in Adwa left nobody behind. Everything was cut off with their defeat, and their death remained purposeless. There they lay, separated from Italy by so much land and sea, and it likewise appeared that they remained separated from the course of Italy's present and future history. Dead for the fatherland, left there without a fatherland. Having died while fulfilling the supreme duty, for them it was as if they had not been born. A part of the Italian people raised loud cries of grief over their misadventure, but the grief only served to bring out a fury of hatred and civil unrest; and thus the final unparalleled havoc done in their name was more horrible than the ferocity of Abyssinian steel upon their bodies. Dead for the fatherland, they served to lacerate the fatherland. Another part of the Italian people, considering them the victims of a huge error, or a huge crime committed by the men of government, shrank in horror at the crime, and shrank from them. And [yet] another part of the

Italian people, for that same love of the fatherland, shrinking at the thought of defeat, of another defeat, shrank [also] at the thought of the defeated. But in the humble homes, in the solitude of families, their mothers and fathers wept over them. For the rest, they had a sepulture in the Adwa valley, so far from Italian territory, so far from Italian history. And that is why their fate appeared to us incomparably sadder than those who had fallen at Custoza, or who at Lissa had sank to the bottom of the sea with their staved ship. Even there, the fatherland watched over them; but over in Adwa, the eyes of the fatherland are closed.

Why, citizens? Why was that year so horrendously sad for us? Why did we have so nefarious a peace?

You know why: not because Italy was beaten by Abyssinia, but because Italy was beaten by Italians. Here, at home – not the Abyssinian victory at Adwa – but here at home, across our one hundred cities, from the peaks of the Alps to the farthest point of Sicily, another victory ran, shouting; here it threw our banner into the mud; here, like the enemy's broken backs, it broke the roads over which reinforcements for the war needed to pass. And it was an Italian victory. It was the victory of Italian indignations over the Italian nation.

It was the victory of a people over one man. The victory of a people that was completely against the nation, over one man in whose heart the entire nation had found refuge.

In the national life of peoples, you are aware,

o citizens, of the clash between the two fasci of forces, the forces by which nations are constituted, preserved, and grow, continuously tending to evolve and expand; and the forces whereby nations tend to turn inward on themselves, to become twisted within themselves, and against themselves, to disintegrate and dissolve, to pass, in more proper and precise terms, from their state of organic unity into classes and the tumult of classes, from this into individuals and the tumult of individuals, reluctantly retracing the path they had taken over the centuries in order to arrive at their constitution. Well, then: in that year of 1896, the entire fascio of national forces had been, as I have said, reduced to the heart of Francesco Crispi, while the rest of Italy was being swept away by anti-national forces.

It was the Italy of the kingdom and the Italy of the people. The Italy of the kingdom, constitutional Italy, that of the so-called parties of order, liberals and moderates, more moderate (a word of debilitation) than liberal (already an empty word); it had already let the other Italy of the people slip from its grasp, already anti-constitutional, democratic, republican, under the hidden and not-hidden dominion of the worst foreign power, France, and primarily socialist in socialism's first blush of youth. And both of them, the Italy of the kingdom and the Italy of the people, had forged an alliance, a conspiracy rather, in parliament, led by two leaders, Felice Cavallotti, the pig iron of republican and pro-French left, and the Marquis Antonio di Rudini, the ultimate vanity of the right.

Against them stood one man, Francesco Crispi. Having returned to power two years earlier, at the end of 1893, listen to what he had to say:

> *At home, rebellion, already erupted in several provinces of the kingdom, in others, latent; the national fabric, disintegrated; the consciousness of unity and even of the very reason for the fatherland's existence, muddled; minds disturbed not only by the evidence of evil, but by fear and presentiment of greater evil, seemingly. Material discomfort on a par with spiritual agitation, for no longer merely large, but also small, inconvenient, bothersome needs: credit depreciated, commerce made more difficult, revenue inadequate to government needs, and the sources of public and private resources depleted through general disorganization. Abroad, surprise at all that, which translated into distrust and discredit, which in turn made the difficulties and internal dangers even greater.*

All that notwithstanding, Francesco Crispi wanted the war of conquest because, even if he had not promoted it, he certainly expanded its designs and scope. Why? What sort of politician was he to have so poorly matched the nation's undertakings to its conditions?

History will say that Francesco Crispi in his

time must have had one destiny alone: that of being a hero and a martyr. History will say that his destiny was to have faith and love for an entire people who no longer had either. History will say that his destiny was to act and suffer for an entire people who no longer wanted him. History will say that his destiny was to be, in himself alone, what an entire people no longer were. History will define the terrible destiny of Francesco Crispi in this way: that he had to be, in and of himself, an organic Italy, one that no longer existed outside of himself, and it had to exist in him because, otherwise, at that time, it would have existed nowhere else. And he answered. Indeed, that faith and love of his were so strong that they alone, for years and years, indefatigably created the nation; by that faith and that love the nation arose and revived, it subsisted in them. In them alone, against both domestic and foreign enemies, it persevered. The tragedy was for the man, who in his labored breath and in the frayed thread of his final days had to bear the entire millennial inspiration and entire weight of the Italian people on his shoulders; the tragedy was for him, when the illusion crashed when he found himself alone, face to face with defeat; but in reality the nation was inside him, completely and entirely inside him; in him it lived, in him it was active. Prodigy of prodigies and tragedy of tragedies, while everywhere outside it was dying; in him, according to the powerful rhythm of the heart that he had, according to the vastness and generosity of the soul that he had, according to faith and love, according to an entire life that was nothing else if not the indefatigable labor of that faith and love amid exile, conspiracies, poverty, and war; prodigy of prodigies, tragedy of tragedies, while outside the nation was dying; in him alone it was evolving according to its eternal laws; with the entire fascio of its eternal forces, it was passing from the stage of its formation and preservation to the stage of its expansion; it was laying the foundations of its empire. In him alone. In him, as in Giuseppe Mazzini, Italy was grieving for having been liberated with the help of foreign arms. In him, as in Nino Bixio and in Vittorio Emanuele, Italy was feeling the need to grow stronger abroad and at home with a war; Italy without victories, with a victorious war. Such a statesman was he! In him, despite his also appearing, since the Italian Revolution, to have imbibed the venom of the French Revolution; in him, Italy immediately turned against what was, for unshakable reasons of affinity and rivalry, geography, demography, and diversity of historical development, in short, everything – what was, is, and will be its constitutional antagonist: France. Such a statesman was he! He had for Italy the necessity for, a true and proper concupiscence for Italian action in international politics, he had a concupiscence for Italian conquest. He had a concupiscence for guarding the Mediterranean against friends and foes alike, and was, for as long as his voice and his eyes held out, its guard dog; and only in his furor of love, and as if in a kind of barbaric jealousy for something of his own that had been stolen from him, did he find the strength to inspire fear both near and far. Such a statesman was he! In 1881 – a statesman like Cairoli he was not – to whom, still swooning in traditional French tendernesses and who continued to delude himself as to the fate of Tunisia, Francesco Crispi shouted: "One must needs have forgotten history to believe that the French army, after having pun-

ished the rebel tribes, will leave Tunisia." And for
Italy that year he felt deeply wounded in the side; he
felt that the equilibrium in the Mediterranean had
been broken on the western flank. And in 1882,
Francesco Crispi – a statesman like Mancini he was
not – felt that same equilibrium broken on the eastern
flank as well, when the English requested the cooperation of Italian arms in Egypt and did not get them.
Then, running between Rome and London, he urged
Mancini first to take up, then to resume, negotiations
with England, saying: "We must intervene in Egypt.
If we should remain inert, France will consolidate its
hold over Tunisia, and Tripolitania will be at risk.
The Mediterranean will be taken away from us forev-
er." And not having any official mission in London,
in a colloquy with Lord Granville he searched long
and hard in Granville's eyes to see whether it was op-
portune to push the agenda. And when Mancini's
"wise inertia" remained steadfastly "no," Francesco
Crispi wrote to him:

> *Would to God that your refusal does
> not cause new harm to Italy in the
> Mediterranean. You ought to have ac-
> cepted without hesitation. When
> Cavour had made the offer to join the
> Western powers in the Crimean War,
> he did not hesitate for one second. The
> small Piedmont government [at that
> time] had the courage that the Italian
> government lacks today.*

And finally, since July 1890, *l'homme bien étonnant*,
as Lord Salisbury called him, in order to reestablish

the equilibrium between Egypt and Tunisia, set his sights on Tripolitania and assayed the thought of London, Berlin, Vienna, and even Paris on the matter; and so as not to waste any time he began to prepare the Arabs and approached one of the faithful Hassuna who became famous eleven years later. And in the latter part of January '91, having left the ministry and returned to it two years later, at seventy-five years of age; after Tunis, after Egypt, after Tripoli, he continued to seek the reestablishment of the equilibrium that had been broken; and once again, rousing Italy with ever greater activity, the hero who overcame both old age and conflicts urged Italy not to be left behind other nations in the historical period of great colonial conquests, but to follow them, and he enlarged the field and design of the Abyssinian war.

He had all the parties against him, those from which he had emerged, and those that he had always fought against; and all the hatred, all the vendettas, all the envy, and, as you may recall, o citizens, the injured, hypocritical, and calumniating morality. All the little nobodies of constituted and constitutional Italy abhorred him, simply because cowardice abhors virtue, and what is miserable and small shrinks from greatness. All that Italy of the kingdom, the state, and parliament, all that Italy of aristocrats, the fat bourgeoisie with unimaginative minds, merchants, communal mayors, university professors, right-minded people; all that Italy that didn't exist twenty years earlier, but which already, having been formed without reforming itself, nor replenishing itself, from the old cultured and seignorial classes of the era of serfdom and division, was now senile; all that Italy of teeming, but ambitious, but avid, but petulant, but politicking little men; all that Italy of Italian little men rose up against the solitary hero, the one Italian who was the entire fatherland, and its future enlargement. And already between that insurrection of the palace and the villa, that conspiracy of the antechamber and the hall, the class struggle broke out in the street, the foreign voice of Karl Marx drowned out at the rallies the Italian voice of Giuseppe Mazzini, which by now could only be found in his books. It was at that time an obscene mix of moderates from yesterday and the violent types of today, anarchists, and monarchists, noblemen with cunning smiles and demagogues who leapt into the piazza with parricidal frenzy. The mayors of large cities, consecrated to institutions on account of birth and wealth, leaned out of municipal windows and, addressing the mutinous hordes, who were pleased finally to be able to hear the benevolent voices in person, said to them: that it was well known, it was well known just how badly they had always considered the African affair to be, and how they would never stop addressing respectful appeals to the government to put an end to it, in the name of the people! – On the assault of all these people and on himself, Francesco Crispi could have thought:

> *The national tribunal has been converted into a place of defamation, parliamentary immunity has been transformed into the inviolability of offense, and the struggle of the people, or rather against the individual, has replaced the contest of principles. Calumny is not a new weapon in poli-*

tics, it has replaced the dagger in democratic countries and medieval poison, and it is resorted to all the more willingly when the stone of some miscalculating David, the bullet of some fanatic assassin, has missed the mark. Never before was it so clamorous, violent, or as insinuating, acute, and comprehensive, crafted with skill, plotted with ability. The disgust that such a war would have awakened in the mind of a man who had reached the end of a long and tiring career, was counted on, and it was supposed in fact to lead to peace. And only if I had ceded, only if I had bowed down before this new system of provoking ministerial crises by means of defamation and had accepted the convenient theory that a minister, however calumniated, must defend himself and, in order to defend himself, let go of power, giving thus to the first of these insulting louts free rein to change how the country is governed, the country would very quickly have seen, with more nausea now than wonder, vituperation newly transformed into hosannas. But it was not just today that I learned to suffer in order to fulfill my duty, and I resisted.

And he resisted, the nearly eighty-year-old man, the hero, turning his love into passion, his conscience into strength, his obstinacy into invincibility.

Until, like Napoleon after Waterloo, having suffered others' failures and his own fate at Adwa, the Italian statesman who actually possessed the Napoleonic power to create and enlarge countries, could no longer resist.

Who won?

Anarchy.

The anarchy that was called the people's will, the anarchy that was called the salvation of the father-land, the anarchy that was called the monarchy, the anarchy that was called the extreme left, the anarchy that was called Di Rudini, the anarchy that was called Cavallotti, the anarchy that went by ten other social-ists' names.

Everything that could with one single word be called anti-nation won.

Four days later, on March 5, at two in the af-ternoon, five minutes transpired in the history of Italy that ought to be called the five infamous minutes. The vanquished hero entered the hall of parliament and said:

"I have the honor of announcing to the house that the ministry has offered its resignation to His Majesty the King."

After a moment of silence, he added, raising his voice:

"His Majesty the King has accepted it."

Applause broke out on the floor and in the galleries, with the shouting of:

"Long live the King!"

But when the extreme left inveighed against the vanquished hero, he turned toward them and, after they had fallen silent, he added:

"The ministers will remain at their posts until their successors are nominated, so as to maintain public order."

Then the martyr was covered in vituperations and called a coward.

In that moment he had reached a low point.

With him, also, the nation had reached a low point.

When did it rise again? When did the Italian nation rise again, after how many years, and how? After a brief or long period of time? When was the beginning of the Risorgimento, and how and why and where?

We do not know: we cannot place it, not in a day, not in a year, not in an event, not in a location. We know only that there was a time when the Italian people remained without the Italian nation, a time when Italy went through national nihilism, a time when we thirty-five million Italians felt ourselves in a diaspora within the very borders of our own territory; like that portion of us who crossed the ocean, we felt like exiles in our own country. Then, if we were reminded that Italy was Italy, or rather, that it was a sin-

gle name that comprised a single population inhabit-
ing a single country, this thing no longer appeared
true to us. If we were reminded that we spoke the
same language, and that for three thousand years we
had the same history, and that for several centuries we
had been under the yoke of the same foreigner, and
that after several decades we had won our independence with the same arms, this thing no longer appeared real to us. If we were reminded that we had an
army and a navy and a state and all the other institutions and laws in common, this thing no longer appeared real to us. We felt an emptiness in all that, as
we did in ourselves, in our thoughts, and even in our
daily work.

How long did it last? How long did it take us
to be convinced, ourselves and others, that the history
of the young kingdom was finished and that only the
disheartening chronicle remained? That foreign politics were precluded us? That we would no longer be
capable of sustaining a war?

We cannot say for sure.

But the day came when the eternal laws that
govern those human societies called nations, having
been enforced; when economic progress, having
come to fruition, if that were the case; when factions,
having been debilitated, if that were the case; when a
more artful government, having produced its effects,
if that were indeed the case; when the same conditions in Europe with their changes, having conspired
together, and the precise facts of European politics,
having awakened its historic destiny; – the day finally
came when we could lift our arms up to heaven, and

our voices, and shout: "Italy has risen again!"

Citizens of Bologna!

That day was September 28, 1911, when the king's government ordered Turkey to cede both Tripolitania and Cyrenaica to Italy within twenty-four hours. It was September 29, when war was declared. They were the days of Tripoli, they were the days of that winter, and that spring of 1912, when all the Italian people were in agreement and that agreement was an enthusiasm, and that enthusiasm was a joy, and that joy was because the Italian nation had finally found itself again. Did we make war? Did we win it? Did we conquer a colony? There was that, but so much more. Who was alive in those days? Who saw the new spark in the eyes of our brothers and sisters; who heard the trembling words on their lips? Who saw the exultant children, and the aged consoled by a beautiful death? Did we make war, I repeat, did we win it, did we conquer a colony? There was that, but so much more. It was the sacred season when so many Italians were alive, regained contact, and reentered into communion with their vibrant national unity. It was the sacred season, o citizens, when the thirty-five million Italians scattered from the loftiest peaks of the Alps to the farthest point of Sicily returned to the fatherland.

And for that reason we may now, as I said at the beginning, not only commemorate, but celebrate our soldiers who died at Adwa.

We can do so because we can celebrate our nation. By now, the expansion of our nation is a *fait accompli*. Adverse forces continue to work against us, but they will not prevail. Sullied by recent suffrage, the successors of those who won in 1896, or they themselves, those who might want to hold Italy back and reduce it to the size of the cooperative of labor under the regimen of the labor union, we hear them, from the seats that they defile, inveighing against Libya, proclaiming the people's will, professing friendship for our enemies, vindicating the Arabs – the Arabs, mind you, not the Italians – vindicating the fallen Arabs at Sciara Sciat. But what else are they capable of besides the nausea they fill us with and the disgust they elicit in us? Libya is a fact. Another fact is our taking up position in Albania, while we expand our occupation in Libya. Our tending towards Asia is a fact, while only just yesterday we descended on Africa. The fact is that Europe senses the expanding movement of this Italy of ours in every direction, and peoples and sovereigns, statesmen and journalists, they all speak about it, asking themselves whether they ought to be concerned and fear it, when they are already concerned and already fear it. The fact is, in summary, o citizens, that Italy is no longer a prey to the forces of its own destruction, but is under the loving guide of the magnificent forces that harmoniously develop it, evolve it, and amplify it. We can now make ourselves a great announcement, from one person to the other, citizens of Bologna: our noble fatherland has already entered into the service of world civilization.

A sovereign law takes the chosen people at the first nucleus of their national formation and, from age to age, continually driving them, inspiring them, and enlarging them, leads them to empire. When empire exists, nations enter into the service of world civilization. They do not know it and they do not need to know it, they act, they wage wars, they add conquest after conquest and believe that in this way they are serving only their egoism, but they serve the cause of the species, the propagation of the species, the expansion of active progress, the diffusion of luminous thought.

Well, citizens, the sovereign law that I have spoken to you about, the law of Rome, is already leading our noble fatherland.

So let us celebrate, let us celebrate those who were the first to spill their blood for it in the Adwa valley.

Let us celebrate their death now that we understand it. Let us celebrate their death now that we know that it was not in vain. The blood of fallen soldiers is like men's seed, it too is generative; but it is like scattered seed, when the battle is lost, the war cut short, and the plan abandoned even. And that is how it was for the dead soldiers at Adwa. But now we know that even if the battle was lost and the war cut short, a secret plan of providence was preserved, and at the proper time it reappeared and had a happy conclusion elsewhere. And therefore those Italian soldiers, whose deaths were fruitful for the fatherland, have now become heroes.

They were like the man for whose will they died: they were the precursors, the man was a precursor.

And, to be honest, now that we understand it, now that we recognize it, the life of this man who suffered so much appears to us to have had a destiny like no other citizen of any other people. For there are three periods in the life of elect nations, as I have mentioned, their rise, their consolidation, and their enlargement and empire; Francesco Crispi was able to see Italy achieve all three, and he was able to be useful in all three periods. Because in the first period, when Italy was destined to be liberated and unified as a nation, having made himself an exile for her, after fleeing his native island, for the peninsula, for Europe, and begging for love of her more than for bread for himself, which he did have need of, he was a counselor of the wisest, an inciter of the most ardent, a persuader of the most decided, a thinker among the most visionary, showing patience among the most obstinate, being a fox among the most astute and a lion among the most powerful. And in the second period, when Italy was a nation, he took control of the state, knowing the art, which he took with him to the grave, of rendering it more liberal and more sound. And before dying he initiated, for Italy, and, by the genius of his heart almost, he generated the third period; he was the precursor, indeed the founder of the Italian empire. He was the founder by the certitude that he carried with him to the grave, in spite of everything. Listen:

> The unity of our fatherland, achieved by the Savoy dynasty and by the Italian people, will be completed in the new century with the prosperity and greatness to which the nation has the

right to aspire. It will be the glory of Your Majesty's reign: reaching the desired goal by all of Italy.

Francesco Crispi sent this letter to the king on December 21, 1900. Several months later, whatever remained of him was fading: a memory to commemorate the past and its certain future. So certain that we today, by order of a justice more real than any factual reality, perceive in the defeat of Adwa a sign pointing to the victory at Tripoli. And so, to summarize and conclude our discourse, o citizens, Francesco Crispi was the statesman of the third Italy, of the same stature as Camillo Cavour. Let us affirm him finally, and against the opinion of those who persist in judging the man by his defeat and condemning him because he could not adjust his ambitions to national possibilities; let us give him a full pardon, and let us hasten with his apotheosis. Thank God for Francesco Crispi! Where would we be without him! In defeat, he prepared us for victory, in abandonment, conquest. While he was leading the undertaking that was thwarted by the fascio of anti-national forces, he sowed the vigorous seed from which the reaction of national forces would eventually rise and then triumph. Thus he paved the way for the consciousness of the new Italy destined to break out of its confines. He was our true and only father. He was guilty of the defeat at Adwa, just as the Savoy dynasty and its ministers were guilty of the war of '48 lost by small Piedmont. But because of this, while they were defeated, they materialized a commitment in themselves and in Piedmont, in Italy, and in Europe even, for the reconquest of '59. And so Francesco Crispi, because of

Adwa, in our most secret and sound and sensitive national fibers, materialized a commitment to allow us to renew ourselves, which was satisfied in 1912. And therefore he truly created the historical destiny, not a European destiny according to today's politicians, but an Italian one, and only an Italian one, in our opinion.

Glory be to him then, and to the young soldiers who collaborated with him, dying in the Adwa valley.

Glory be to them, more than in any other city, in this Bologna; glory be as well to two other great spirits that are present here today. For when Francesco Crispi fell, and all those who hadn't persecuted him abandoned him, and all those who had understood him no longer understood him, and the fatherland and the world were against him, two men had the heart to draw near him and stand by him and sanctify his greatness in misfortune. They were the poet whom you cared for on Italy's behalf, citizens of Bologna, and the historian who lived in the vicinity with his ire and his solitude which made him greater than himself.

Having passed away, they too, before the changing of the times, they could have had more love than faith, and seemed to bow their reluctant heads in death, asking themselves: "Why were we born?" Because if the old saying is true that the citizens of a glorious fatherland are happy, then those born to represent ideal causes in an inglorious fatherland are infinitely unhappy.

But today, since we are granted the opportunity to commemorate the mourning of Adwa with the joy of Tripoli, the spirit of poetry and the spirit of history also return and radiate in the new life of the fatherland, exulting because they can finally celebrate it.

Glory, glory to those who died for the fatherland, glory too to those who suffered for the fatherland! Glory to all, statesman and soldiers! Glory to everyone, to those who lay down at Adwa with defeat, and to those who lay down in Libya with victory! Because the two wars can be considered as two phases of a single war: the war for Italy's advancement in the world.

Glory then to all without distinction!

And if there is some father or mother in this city who remembers their son fallen in today's or yesterday's battles, may they be honored by you. And if there is anyone still alive who fought before, or after, may he be honored by you.

Glory, glory to all who died for the fatherland, glory to all who suffered for the fatherland! Glory to those who worked for the enlargement of the fatherland and, with the passing of time, an ever greater glory in an ever greater fatherland whose workers will be the brothers who come after.

Other Books by the Publisher

Fanchette's Pretty Little Foot by Restif de La Bretonne

Je M'Accuse... by Léon Bloy

My Hospitals & My Prisons by Paul Verlaine

Salvation Through the Jews by Léon Bloy

Words of a Demolitions Contractor by Léon Bloy

Cellulely by Paul Verlaine

Ecclesiastical Laurels by Jacques Rochette de la Morlière

Flowers of Bitumen by Émile Goudeau

Songs for Her & Odes in Her Honor by Paul Verlaine

On Huysmans' Tomb by Léon Bloy

Ten Years a Bohemian by Émile Goudeau

The Soul of Napoleon by Léon Bloy

Blood of the Poor by Léon Bloy

Joan of Arc and Germany by Léon Bloy

A Platonic Love by Paul Alexis

The Revealer of the Globe: Christopher Columbus & His Future Beatification (Part One) by Léon Bloy

An Immodest Proposal by Dr. Helmut Schleppend

The Pornographer by Restif de La Bretonne

Style (Theory and History) by Ernest Hello

On the Threshold of the Apocalypse: 1913-1915 by Léon Bloy

She Who Weeps (Our Lady of La Salette) by Léon Bloy

The Sylph by Claude Prosper Jolyot de Crébillon (*fils*)

Voyage in France by a Frenchman by Paul Verlaine

Ourigan, Oregon by William Clark, Richard Robinson, and anonymous

Drowning by Yu Dafu

Cull of April by Francis Vielé-Griffin

The Misfortune of Monsieur Fraque by Paul Alexis

Fêtes Galantes & Songs Without Words by Paul Verlaine

Joys by Francis Vielé-Griffin

The Son of Louis XVI by Léon Bloy

Septentrion by Jean Raspail

The Resurrection of Villiers de l'Isle-Adam by Léon Bloy

Poems Saturnian by Paul Verlaine

The Biography of Léon Bloy: Memories of a Friend by René Martineau

Fredegund, France: A Book of Poetry by Richard Robinson

The Good Song by Paul Verlaine

Swans by Francis Vielé-Griffin

Constantinople and Byzantium by Léon Bloy

Enamels and Cameos by Théophile Gautier

Four Years of Captivity in Cochons-sur-Marne: 1900-1904 by Léon Bloy

Dark Minerva: Prolegomena: The Moral Construction of Dante's Divine Comedy by Giovanni Pascoli

What is Fascism: Discourses and Polemics by Giovanni Gentile

The Desperate Man by Léon Bloy

Meditations of a Solitary in 1916 by Léon Bloy

The Ride of Yeldis & Other Poems by Francis Vielé-Griffin

Silvie & The Chimeras by Gérard de Nerval